Political
ATLAS·OF
ILLINOIS

Paul Kleppner, Director
Social Science Research Institute

Richard E. Dahlberg, Director
Laboratory for Cartography and
Spatial Analysis

Ruth Anne Tobias
Center for Governmental Studies

Kevin M. Himmelberger
Social Science Research Institute

Richard P. Vaupel
Laboratory for Cartography and
Spatial Analysis

Northern Illinois University Press · DeKalb, Illinois ·1988

ISBN 0-87580-136-6   LC 87-24765

© 1988 by Northern Illinois University Press
Published by the Northern Illinois University Press, DeKalb, Illinois 60115
Manufactured in the United States of America
Design by Anne Schedler

Acknowledgments

It is always a pleasure to recognize publicly the persons who contributed to bringing a scholarly enterprise to fruition. This is especially so in the present instance, since what occurred illustrates quite well how colleagues—both faculty and administrators—can cooperate to achieve common goals. Without that shared commitment, this project would not have been accomplished.

The idea for an atlas of this sort emerged from discussions among several faculty at Northern Illinois University's Social Science Research Institute (SSRI). Each wanted to tackle some research problem that required relating election returns for state legislative districts to census characteristics, but they were frustrated by the preliminary need to work out the linkage between political and census geographies. This was a task that would be tedious, time consuming, and expensive; the sort of activity that could better be taken collectively. With support from the SSRI, Robert Albritton, Research Associate, Center for Governmental Studies, supervised the tasks of building machine-readable files of election returns and then matching these with census data. Anthony Gierzynski, who was then a graduate student in NIU's Department of Political Science, and Kevin Himmelberger, Research Associate, SSRI, painstakingly determined which census units were contained within each political district and then developed matched files of election returns and demographic information. In the process, they received invaluable support from the staff of the Census Data laboratory, Center for Governmental Studies, and from the staffs of the Illinois State Board of Elections and the Board of Election Commissioners, City of Chicago.

Accomplishing these tasks satisfied immediate needs, while giving rise to the notion that the results should be shared more broadly. It was at this point that development and publication of an atlas came under active consideration. Of course, the major problem was locating sufficient funding to cover the cartography and publication costs. L. Douglas Dobson, Director, Center for Governmental Studies, resolved one part of this problem by offering to share the costs of the cartographic work with the SSRI. At a later point, and when it was critically needed, Jerrold H. Zar, Associate Provost for Research and Dean of the Graduate School, made a very timely

iii

contribution to these costs. John E. LaTourette, President of Northern Illinois University, agreed to cover some of the printing costs, and James D. Norris, Dean of the College of Liberal Arts and Sciences, also contributed to defraying these expenses.

With these matters settled, planning and production activities moved forward. The staff of the Laboratory for Cartography and Spatial Analysis—particularly, Mark Howland, Lisa Paulson, and Leonard Walther—made important contributions at numerous points during these processes. The Cart Lab merits praise both for the exceptional quality of its work and for managing to keep its activities on schedule. The staff of the NIU Press also provided valuable assistance, especially Anne Schedler, designer, whose creative talents are apparent on these pages.

Finally, we want to recognize the important contribution of Sandra Petit. She did the initial word processing, somehow squeezing this work in while doing dozens of other tasks and always managing to complete things quickly yet with great accuracy.

Introduction

Information resources in Illinois are generally underdeveloped. Practitioners, participants, and interested citizens often are unable to locate basic information without engaging in major research efforts on their own. As a result, some quickly give up the effort, basing their decisions on intuitive understanding of bits and pieces of information, rather than on analysis of a complete range of data. Others pursue the effort to a conclusion, squandering resources in the process by covering the same ground as still other independent researchers.

The lack of an accessible data base is nowhere more apparent than in the domain of political statistics. The *Illinois Blue Book,* which is published by the state, contains too little political information and virtually no matching demographic data. Moreover, unlike states such as Michigan and New Jersey, there are no regular publications that provide supplemental information to fill these gaps. At the same time, however, the demand for these types of information is growing rapidly, as officeholders, candidates, campaign consultants, pollsters, newspaper and television reporters, and interested citizens try to chart the political outlooks of constituency groups.

The *Political Atlas of Illinois* represents a first step toward filling this informational void. It focuses especially on the state's legislative districts, offering both detailed maps and statistical profiles of each of its 59 senate and 118 house districts. It also includes statewide summary maps depicting political and demographic data both for these districts and for the state's counties. Finally, there are maps showing the political and demographic characteristics of the wards of Chicago.

The central feature of this atlas is its presentation of both maps and statistical snapshots of the state's senate and house districts. Compilations of this sort typically must limit themselves to a few bits of statistical information to supplement the cartographic displays. This is because the census data were not originally collected and reported at the appropriate level of political geography. We were able to do more here because we matched the different geographies. That is, we identified which census units—tracts and blocks in urban areas and townships and counties elsewhere—were contained within each political district, enabling us to exploit the richness of the census files to develop more complete statistical portraits.

Even so, the law of available data operates to limit the presentation. So did the fact that Illinois reapportioned its legislature, shifted from multiple- to single-member districts and reduced the number of legislators after 1980. These changes combined to alter the previous boundaries rather drastically and restricted "historical" comparisons to elections since 1982.

The details concerning data sources and calculations are provided in an appendix, but it will aid understanding to draw attention to some matters here.

Faced with a practical choice between presenting absolute or proportionate values for the demographic data, we opted for a mixture of the two. This reflected our judgment that neither way of measuring was inherently "better" than the other, but that each had its own legitimate uses. So we decided to present for each category the proportionate breakdown along with the absolute number that served as the denominator for calculating the percentages. Thus, for any category of demographic information, readers can reconstruct the absolute value associated with each of the percentages simply by multiplying the number associated with the category's denominator by the appropriate percentage.

We also had to make a tactical decision concerning how to present the political data. It consumed too much space to present the percentages for both major parties, and the two almost invariably summed to unity in any case. On the other hand, we did not want to appear to prefer one party by always presenting its percentage and ignoring the strength of its major opposition. We resolved this minor conundrum by opting to present the percentage for the party of the winning candidate. Thus, the **D** or **R** that follows this percentage in the table indicates whether a Democratic or Republican candidate carried the district in that year, while the designation **N E** for a senate district indicates that no election was held in that district in that year.

We followed the same principle in constructing the summary maps. That is, we presented the percentages for the party that "won" the election in the jurisdiction presented. For example, we used the percentages for the Democrats for the house summary maps since that party won a majority of seats statewide in the elections presented. But we mapped the Republican percentages for president because that party's candidates carried the state in the three elections reviewed. Similarly, we presented the Democratic percentages for state and county offices in Chicago because Democratic candidates outpolled their Republican opponents in the city even when losing in larger jurisdictions.

Finally, the graphics depicting immigrant-stock population presented as sidebar material for some districts take only European and Asian sources of the population into account. That is, the immigrant-stock population *excludes* immigrants from Mexico, Cuba, and Central and South America.

Only two types of data arrayed on the summary maps require any additional comment. The index of party competition was calculated by taking the absolute difference between the percentages of the vote cast for the Democrats and Republicans. Thus, an even division of the vote between the two major parties produces an index value of zero, while a value of 100 indicates that one party captured all of the votes. Second, where we have presented the "Democratic" percentage of the vote for governor and secretary of state in the 1986 general election, the returns are those for the Illinois Solidarity Party. This was the label under which regular Democrats ran for these offices after disciples of the political extremist Lyndon LaRouche unexpectedly won the party's nominations for two offices in the March primary. However, for other state, county, and legislative offices, regular Democrats ran under the party's traditional label.

Since an atlas is essentially a book of maps rather than a text illustrated by maps, we have consciously chosen not to offer an extended commentary describing either the shape or trends of Illinois politics. But a few political patterns—for the state and for Chicago—do merit notice.

First, most of the state's house and senate districts are not very competitive politically. Over the past three elections, the average difference between the candidates of the major parties has been under ten percentage points in only 6.7 percent of the house districts, while it has been thirty percentage points or more in 67.8 percent of them. The corresponding figures for Senate races are only marginally better—8.5 percent with less than a ten-point difference and 62.7 percent won by thirty points or more.

Second, relatively few of the state's counties have been politically noncompetitive in recent gubernatorial and presidential elections. Over the past three contests of each type, the average difference between the major parties has been thirty percentage points or more in only 18.3 percent of the state's counties in presidential elections and in 17.3 percent in gubernatorial races, but it has been under ten percentage points in 24.0 percent of them in both types of contests.

Third, comparisons of the political and demographic data for Chicago's mayoral elections in 1983 and 1987 show the sharp racial polarization that has emerged there.

Fourth, the data for the 1986 Democratic primary in Chicago show how weak organizational loyalty has become as a cue to voting in what was a machine-dominated city. Only ten wards supported all four slated candidates, and ten more supported three of the four, while twenty-one wards rejected all four. Significantly, eighteen of these twenty-one wards have a voting age population that is predominantly black.

Fifth, in the 1986 general election, the black wards were more reliably Democratic than any other group of wards in Chicago. Indeed, even Richard Elrod, the incumbent Sheriff of Cook County and losing Democratic candidate for reelection, polled over 70.0 percent of the vote in each of the city's nineteen predominantly black wards.

Sixth, the index of support for Trustees of the University of Illinois, which is based on sums of the votes cast for all three positions, can be interpreted as a proxy for party identification. If so, then the results indicate that there was a wide gap between underlying party attachments and actual voting selections in most of Chicago's wards in 1986, and the difference was especially noticeable in the wards with a majority of white voting age population.

Contents

Legislative
D I S T R I C T S

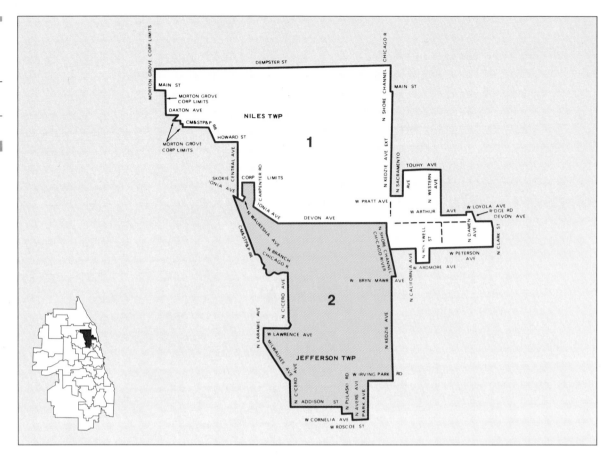

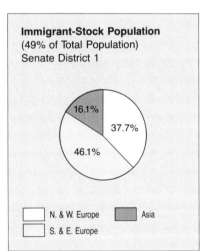

Immigrant-Stock Population
(49% of Total Population)
Senate District 1

37.7%
16.1%
46.1%

☐ N. & W. Europe   ▨ Asia
☐ S. & E. Europe

House District 1 includes most of
the community of West Ridge and
a small part of Uptown in Chicago,
along with Lincolnwood and most
of Skokie in Cook County.

House District 2 contains most of
Albany Park, North Park, and Irving Park, about half of Forest Glen,
and small slices of Avondale and
Portage Park.

	H.D. 1	H.D. 2	S.D. 1
Voting Age Population	**81,148**	**78,720**	**159,868**
White	91.5%	85.3%	88.5%
Black	.3%	.2%	.3%
Hispanic	2.8%	7.9%	5.3%
Asian	5.3%	6.5%	5.9%
Age (Total Population)	**96,473**	**96,251**	**192,724**
Under 6	5.7%	7.4%	6.5%
6 to 18	15.6%	17.3%	16.3%
65 and Over	17.9%	15.2%	16.6%
Education (Age 25 and over)	**67,284**	**61,601**	**128,885**
Less than 12 Years	25.7%	38,1%	31,6%
16 Years or More	27.0%	17.9%	22.7%
Urban Population	**100.0%**	**100.0%**	**100.0%**
Family Income (Total Families)	**27,724**	**24,916**	**52,640**
Median Income	$28,028	$25,865	$25,571
Below Poverty Level	1.9%	2.8%	2.3%
With Children Under 6	.5%	1.3%	.9%
With Children 6 to 17	1.1%	2.3%	1.7%
Headed by Females	.1%	.4%	.2%
Industry (Total Employed)	**53,258**	**48,378**	**101,636**
Professional/Public Admin.	27.2%	22.9%	25.2%
Manufacturing	20.2%	27.8%	23.8%
Retail	19.2%	15.5%	17.4%
Transportation/Communication	4.2%	6.3%	5.2%
Finance/Insurance/Real Estate	9.3%	9.1%	9.2%
Other Service	8.9%	8.9%	8.9%
Housing Units (Total)	**38,116**	**37,997**	**76,113**
Median Value	$82,865	$68,119	$75,492
Owner Occupied	60.4%	45.2%	52.8%
Election Results			
1982 Turnout	43.3%	33.2%	43.3%
Winner	74.9% D	100.0% D	71.4% D
1984 Turnout	53.3%	46.3%	49.6%
Winner	62.9% D	62.6% D	63.8% D
1986 Turnout	37.5%	33.6%	N E
Winner	66.4% D	72.3% D	N E

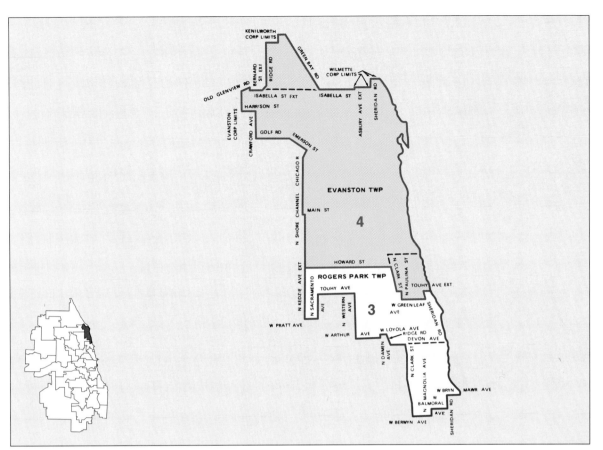

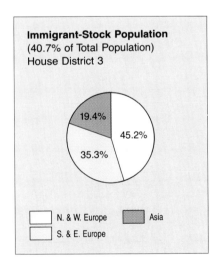

Immigrant-Stock Population
(40.7% of Total Population)
House District 3

45.2%	
35.3%	
19.4%	

☐ N. & W. Europe   ▨ Asia
☐ S. & E. Europe

Most of Uptown is in House District 3, along with smaller pieces of Rogers Park and West Ridge.

The rest of Rogers Park, all of Evanston Township, and a small fraction of New Trier Township are in House District 4.

	H.D. 3	H.D. 4	S.D. 2
Voting Age Population	**85,657**	**73,502**	**159,159**
White	76.6%	76.5%	76.6%
Black	7.8%	17.3%	12.2%
Hispanic	8.4%	3.7%	6.2%
Asian	6.9%	2.5%	4.9%
Age (Total Population)	**96,250**	**96,581**	**192,831**
Under 6	5.9%	6.0%	6.0%
6 to 18	11.5%	15.9%	13.7%
65 and Over	17.9%	14.4%	16.1%
Education (Age 25 and over)	**66,118**	**60,502**	**126,620**
Less than 12 Years	25.9%	17.7%	22.0%
16 Years or More	29.1%	41.4%	35.0%
Urban Population	**100.0%**	**100.0%**	**100.0%**
Family Income (Total Families)	**21,571**	**20,845**	**42,416**
Median Income	$20,694	$27,044	$23,574
Below Poverty Level	4.6%	2.3%	3.5%
With Children Under 6	2.8%	1.2%	2.0%
With Children 6 to 17	2.3%	1.7%	2.0%
Headed by Females	1.1%	.6%	.9%
Industry (Total Employed)	**53,361**	**47,705**	**101,066**
Professional/Public Admin.	30.3%	40.2%	35.0%
Manufacturing	18.5%	14.4%	16.6%
Retail	16.4%	12.9%	14.8%
Transportation/Communication	5.1%	5.0%	5.0%
Finance/Insurance/Real Estate	11.4%	11.0%	11.2%
Other Service	10.5%	10.8%	10.7%
Housing Units (Total)	**50,707**	**40,079**	**90,786**
Median Value	$70,035	$94,404	$82,219
Owner Occupied	23.6%	39.8%	30.7%
Election Results			
1982 Turnout	35.2%	44.5%	30.3%
Winner	78.1% D	62.0% D	100.0% D
1984 Turnout	28.1%	49.1%	N E
Winner	100.0% D	64.1% D	N E
1986 Turnout	27.4%	34.5%	31.0%
Winner	79.4% D	68.5% D	73.2% D

3rd
Senate
DISTRICT

House District 5
House District 6

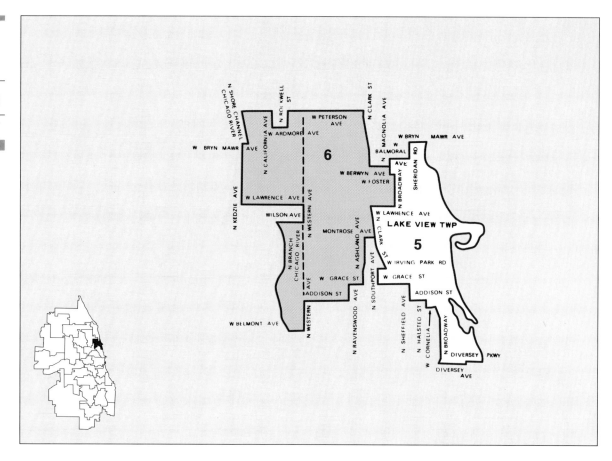

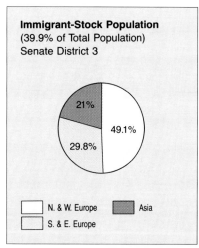

Immigrant-Stock Population
(39.9% of Total Population)
Senate District 3

- 49.1%
- 21%
- 29.8%

☐ N. & W. Europe ▨ Asia
☐ S. & E. Europe

Most of Edgewater, nearly half of Lake View, and a small part of Uptown make up House District 5.

Large portions of Lincoln Square and North Center are in House District 6, along with small slices of Albany Park, Edgewater, Lake View, North Park, Uptown, and West Ridge.

	H.D. 5	H.D. 6	S.D. 3
Voting Age Population	**84,954**	**78,026**	**162,980**
White	69.8%	77.7%	73.6%
Black	11.8%	.7%	6.5%
Hispanic	11.2%	13.4%	12.2%
Asian	6.7%	8.2%	7.4%
Age (Total Population)	**96,908**	**96,471**	**193,379**
Under 6	6.5%	7.5%	7.0%
6 to 18	10.6%	15.9%	13.2%
65 and Over	18.1%	15.9%	17.0%
Education (Age 25 and over)	**69,735**	**63,223**	**132,958**
Less than 12 Years	28.5%	39.2%	33.6%
16 Years or More	31.6%	15.6%	24.0%
Urban Population	**100.0%**	**100.0%**	**100.0%**
Family Income (Total Families)	**18,163**	**24,038**	**42,201**
Median Income	$18,495	$20,009	$19,430
Below Poverty Level	7.2%	3.9%	5.3%
With Children Under 6	4.2%	1.8%	2.8%
With Children 6 to 17	5.2%	2.5%	3.7%
Headed by Females	1.9%	.7%	1.2%
Industry (Total Employed)	**50,593**	**45,861**	**96,454**
Professional/Public Admin.	31.6%	23.6%	27.8%
Manufacturing	18.1%	27.4%	22.5%
Retail	13.1%	16.4%	14.7%
Transportation/Communication	5.8%	6.4%	6.1%
Finance/Insurance/Real Estate	11.8%	8.8%	10.4%
Other Service	12.5%	8.9%	10.8%
Housing Units (Total)	**60,843**	**41,605**	**102,448**
Median Value	$97,233	$56,341	$76,787
Owner Occupied	17.1%	28.0%	21.5%
Election Results			
1982 Turnout	28.4%	29.7%	29.9%
Winner	100.0% D	100.0% D	100.0% D
1984 Turnout	38.8%	38.8%	N E
Winner		60.0% D	N E
1986 Turnout		30.4%	28.3%
Winner		55.4% D	71.7% D

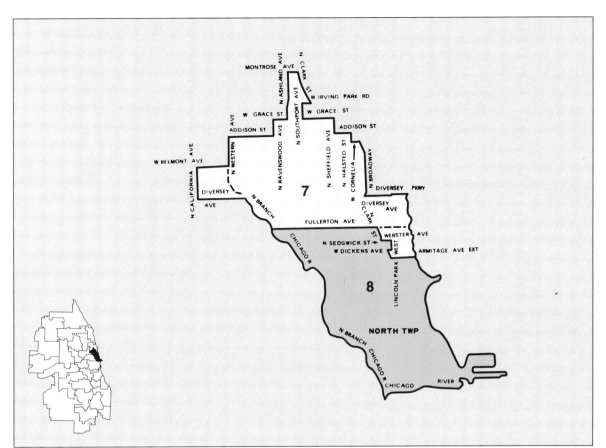

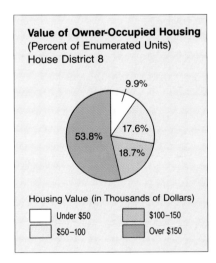

Value of Owner-Occupied Housing
(Percent of Enumerated Units)
House District 8

9.9%

53.8%

17.6%

18.7%

Housing Value (in Thousands of Dollars)

☐ Under $50	▨ $100–150
▥ $50–100	▦ Over $150

House District 7 encompasses about four-tenths of Lake View and North Center, a third of Lincoln Park, and about one-tenth of Avondale.

The rest of Lincoln Park and all of the Near North Side are in House District 8.

The median value of housing units in House District 8 ranks it first in Illinois, but the district also ranks eleventh in the proportion of families below the poverty level.

	H.D. 7	H.D. 8	S.D. 4
Voting Age Population	**85,398**	**79,195**	**164,573**
White	75.7%	76.5%	76.0%
Black	3.5%	18.0%	10.5%
Hispanic	16.6%	4.0%	10.5%
Asian	4.0%	1.5%	2.8%
Age (Total Population)	**97,086**	**96,483**	**193,569**
Under 6	7.2%	6.2%	6.7%
6 to 18	14.2%	12.4%	13.3%
65 and Over	10.8%	11.3%	11.1%
Education (Age 25 and over)	**63,994**	**67,049**	**131,043**
Less than 12 Years	35.1%	18.0%	26.4%
16 Years or More	30.3%	46.3%	38.5%
Urban Population	**100.0%**	**100.0%**	**100.0%**
Family Income (Total Families)	**20,229**	**17,725**	**37,954**
Median Income	$19,308	$24,536	$20,289
Below Poverty Level	5.8%	10.5%	8.0%
With Children Under 6	2.9%	4.0%	3.4%
With Children 6 to 17	4.6%	7.4%	5.9%
Headed by Females	1.5%	6.7%	3.9%
Industry (Total Employed)	**54,012**	**53,473**	**107,485**
Professional/Public Admin.	29.2%	33.3%	31.2%
Manufacturing	21.8%	12.9%	17.4%
Retail	14.1%	12.9%	13.5%
Transportation/Communication	6.6%	6.5%	6.6%
Finance/Insurance/Real Estate	9.6%	14.2%	11.9%
Other Service	11.6%	13.9%	12.7%
Housing Units (Total)	**50,833**	**58,902**	**109,735**
Median Value	$ 44,678	$163,750	$104,214
Owner Occupied	21.4%	23.8%	22.7%
Election Results			
1982 Turnout	29.8%	43.9%	32.2%
Winner	88.2% D	56.4% D	100.0% D
1984 Turnout	41.0%	56.0%	35.3%
Winner	65.2% D	58.1% D	100.0% D
1986 Turnout	25.6%	36.1%	N E
Winner	76.2% D	61.1% D	N E

5th
Senate
DISTRICT

House District 9
House District 10

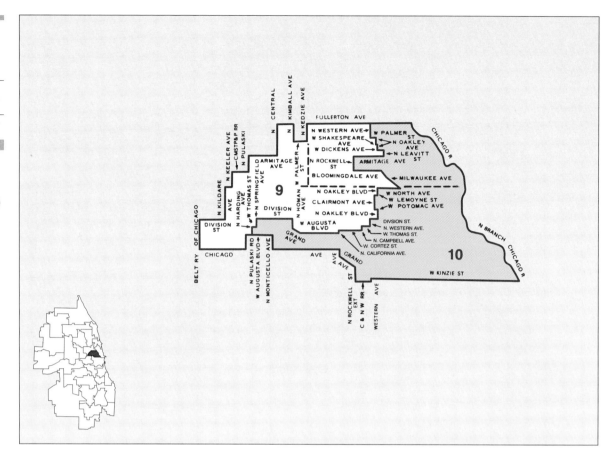

Nearly half of Humboldt Park, about a third of Logan Square and West Town, and a small slice of Hermosa make up House District 9.

Most of West Town, another third of Logan Square, and a small fraction of Humboldt Park are in House District 10.

Senate District 5 is among the state's poorest districts. Its median income is the fourth lowest; over nine-tenths of its owner-occupied housing is valued at less that $50,000; it ranks fifth in the percentage of families below the poverty level; and the proportion of its population failing to complete high school is higher than any other district in Illinois.

	H.D. 9	H.D. 10	S.D. 5
Voting Age Population	78,388	71,811	150,199
White	48.1%	53.2%	50.5%
Black	5.3%	9.2%	7.2%
Hispanic	45.1%	36.7%	41.1%
Asian	1.6%	.8%	1.2%
Age (Total Population)	96,896	96,170	193,066
Under 6	13.5%	12.0%	12.7%
6 to 18	26.0%	23.0%	24.5%
65 and Over	6.9%	8.9%	7.9%
Education (Age 25 and over)	46,856	50,596	97,452
Less than 12 Years	69.9%	66.2%	67.9%
16 Years or More	5.7%	6.4%	6.1%
Urban Population	100.0%	100.0%	100.0%
Family Income (Total Families)	22,099	22,265	44,364
Median Income	$13,690	$14,040	$13,861
Below Poverty Level	13.2%	10.7%	11.9%
With Children Under 6	6.9%	5.6%	6.2%
With Children 6 to 17	9.2%	7.1%	8.2%
Headed by Females	5.9%	4.0%	5.0%
Industry (Total Employed)	34,379	34,294	68,673
Professional/Public Admin.	14.9%	16.5%	15.7%
Manufacturing	45.9%	41.9%	43.9%
Retail	13.7%	14.6%	14.1%
Transportation/Communication	6.5%	6.0%	6.3%
Finance/Insurance/Real Estate	4.7%	5.4%	5.1%
Other Service	7.3%	8.6%	7.9%
Housing Units (Total)	34,503	37,173	71,676
Median Value	$26,269	$25,686	$25,977
Owner Occupied	25.7%	21.8%	23.6%
Election Results			
1982 Turnout	26.2%	30.5%	28.8%
Winner	100.0% D	100.0% D	100.0% D
1984 Turnout	21.0%	23.3%	N E
Winner	100.0% D	100.0% D	N E
1986 Turnout	15.5%	21.0%	19.7%
Winner	100.0% D	84.2% D	80.2% D

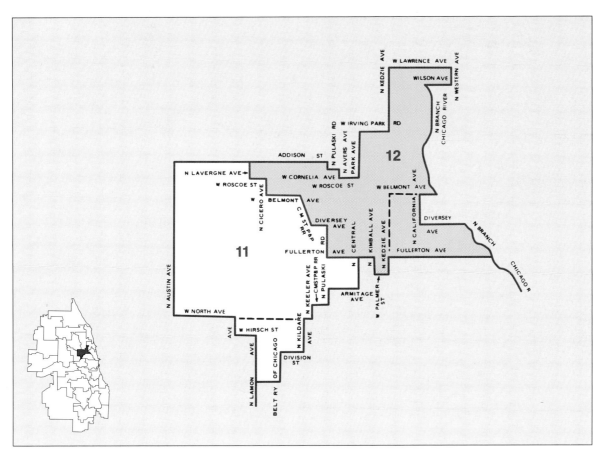

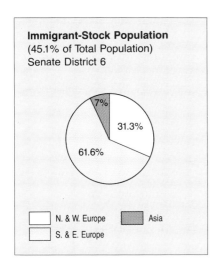

Immigrant-Stock Population
(45.1% of Total Population)
Senate District 6

7%
31.3%
61.6%

| | N. & W. Europe | Asia |
| S. & E. Europe | |

House District 11 covers the major portions of Belmont-Cragin and Hermosa, as well as small parts of Austin, Humboldt Park, Logan Square, and Portage Park.

Most of Avondale, sizable portions of Irving Park and Logan Square, and small sections of Albany Park, Lincoln Square, and Portage Park are in House District 12.

	H.D. 11	H.D. 12	S.D. 6
Voting Age Population	77,468	77,591	155,059
White	83.8%	77.0%	80.4%
Black	2.0%	.4%	1.2%
Hispanic	12.6%	19.1%	15.9%
Asian	1.6%	3.5%	2.5%
Age (Total Population)	95,849	96,104	191,953
Under 6	7.8%	8.7%	8.3%
6 to 18	17.4%	17.5%	17.4%
65 and Over	16.0%	13.1%	14.5%
Education (Age 25 and over)	61,936	60,090	122,026
Less than 12 Years	52.0%	48.5%	50.2%
16 Years or More	7.6%	9.8%	8.7%
Urban Population	100.0%	100.0%	100.0%
Family Income (Total Families)	25,513	24,021	49,534
Median Income	$21,109	$19,105	$20,132
Below Poverty Level	3.4%	5.1%	4.2%
With Children Under 6	1.5%	1.9%	1.7%
With Children 6 to 17	2.1%	2.9%	2.5%
Headed by Females	1.0%	1.2%	1.1%
Industry (Total Employed)	44,938	43,948	88,886
Professional/Public Admin.	16.4%	17.7%	17.0%
Manufacturing	37.9%	36.8%	37.3%
Retail	15.5%	14.6%	15.0%
Transportation/Communication	6.8%	6.4%	6.6%
Finance/Insurance/Real Estate	7.5%	7.4%	7.4%
Other Service	7.0%	7.9%	7.5%
Housing Units (Total)	38,245	39,239	77,484
Median Value	$50,311	$45,795	$48,053
Owner Occupied	47.4%	32.3%	39.7%
Election Results			
1982 Turnout	31.5%	25.5%	30.3%
Winner	100.0% D	100.0% D	100.0% D
1984 Turnout	39.9%	32.9%	N E
Winner	63.4% D	64.1% D	N E
1986 Turnout	21.9%	24.9%	27.6%
Winner	100.0% D	72.1% D	76.8% D

7th
Senate
DISTRICT

House District 13
House District 14

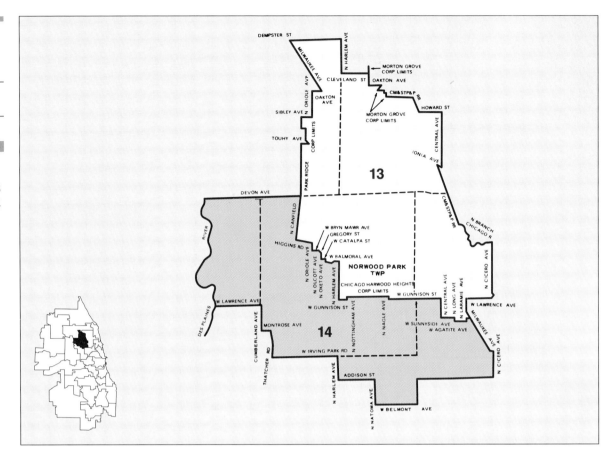

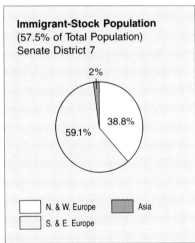

Immigrant-Stock Population
(57.5% of Total Population)
Senate District 7

2%
38.8%
59.1%

☐ N. & W. Europe   ▨ Asia
☐ S. & E. Europe

All of Jefferson Park, most of Edison Park and Norwood Park, almost half of Forest Glen, and slices of Portage Park, Maine, and Niles Townships are in House District 13.

Two-thirds of Portage Park, just under half of Dunning, almost a third of Norwood Park, and small parts of O'Hare and Leyden Township are contained in House District 14.

	H.D. 13	H.D. 14	S.D. 7
Voting Age Population	68,448	65,220	133,668
White	98.8%	97.6%	98.3%
Black	.0%	.4%	.2%
Hispanic	.7%	1.4%	1.1%
Asian	.5%	.5%	.5%
Age (Total Population)	96,567	96,062	192,629
Under 6	4.4%	4.9%	4.7%
6 to 18	16.1%	16.6%	16.4%
65 and Over	19.6%	15.7%	17.6%
Education (Age 25 and over)	67,444	64,700	132,144
Less than 12 Years	36.5%	37.1%	36.8%
16 Years or More	12.9%	10.6%	11.8%
Urban Population	100.0%	100.0%	100.0%
Family Income (Total Families)	27,280	26,431	53,711
Median Income	$27,007	$25,584	$26,292
Below Poverty Level	1.2%	1.3%	1.3%
With Children Under 6	.2%	.2%	.2%
With Children 6 to 17	.6%	.8%	.7%
Headed by Females	.1%	.1%	.1%
Industry (Total Employed)	50,477	47,843	97,960
Professional/Public Admin.	23.1%	18.8%	21.1%
Manufacturing	26.8%	27.0%	26.9%
Retail	15.5%	16.7%	16.1%
Transportation/Communication	8.6%	8.7%	8.7%
Finance/Insurance/Real Estate	9.0%	9.8%	9.4%
Other Service	6.8%	8.1%	7.4%
Housing Units (Total)	37,311	37,399	74,710
Median Value	$70,999	$69,048	$70,023
Owner Occupied	73.6%	63.8%	68.7%
Election Results			
1982 Turnout	59.8%	56.7%	59.1%
Winner	65.2% D	50.8% R	67.7% D
1984 Turnout	73.1%	70.2%	72.6%
Winner	57.1% D	61.2% R	57.5% R
1986 Turnout	56.8%	50.9%	N E
Winner	63.8% D	63.5% R	N E

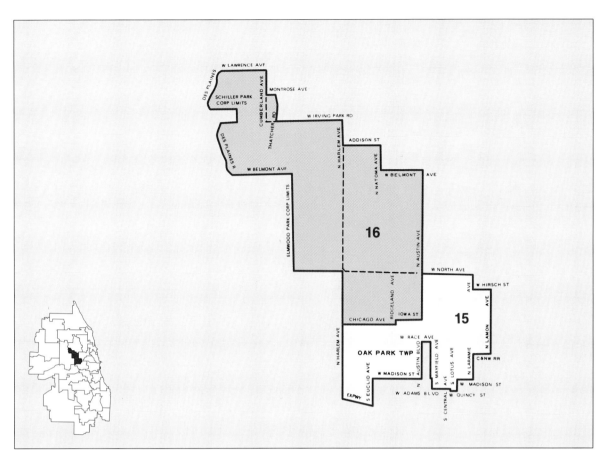

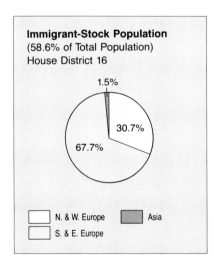

Immigrant-Stock Population
(58.6% of Total Population)
House District 16

1.5%
30.7%
67.7%

N. & W. Europe ☐   Asia ■
S. & E. Europe ☐

House District 15 consists of about 40 percent of both Austin and Oak Park.

All of Mont Clare, half of Dunning, three-tenths of Oak Park, and smaller portions of Austin, Belmont-Cragin, O'Hare, and Leyden Township make up House District 16.

	H.D. 15	H.D. 16	S.D. 8
Voting Age Population	**69,172**	**69,992**	**139,164**
White	33.0%	97.3%	65.3%
Black	61.8%	.7%	31.1%
Hispanic	3.3%	1.7%	2.5%
Asian	1.8%	.4%	1.1%
Age (Total Population)	**97,308**	**95,957**	**193,265**
Under 6	11.1%	5.6%	8.4%
6 to 18	24.8%	16.8%	20.8%
65 and Over	7.5%	18.1%	12.8%
Education (Age 25 and over)	**50,313**	**65,617**	**115,930**
Less than 12 Years	39.0%	39.0%	39.0%
16 Years or More	18.2%	13.5%	15.5%
Urban Population	**100.0%**	**100.0%**	**100.0%**
Family Income (Total Families)	**21,630**	**26,990**	**48,620**
Median Income	$18,110	$25,495	$22,241
Below Poverty Level	9.4%	1.7%	5.2%
With Children Under 6	4.0%	.3%	2.0%
With Children 6 to 17	7.1%	1.1%	3.8%
Headed by Females	5.8%	.2%	2.7%
Industry (Total Employed)	**41,740**	**46,731**	**88,471**
Professional/Public Admin.	29.2%	21.6%	25.1%
Manufacturing	27.0%	27.4%	27.2%
Retail	12.4%	17.8%	15.2%
Transportation/Communication	9.8%	7.6%	8.6%
Finance/Insurance/Real Estate	7.6%	8.0%	7.8%
Other Service	7.7%	7.8%	7.7%
Housing Units (Total)	**35,744**	**37,332**	**73,076**
Median Value	$44,286	$66,468	$55,377
Owner Occupied	31.9%	69.3%	51.0%
Election Results			
1982 Turnout	38.7%	56.4%	48.8%
Winner	80.8% D	54.5% D	74.1% D
1984 Turnout	42.5%	61.5%	N E
Winner	81.5% D	53.2% D	N E
1986 Turnout	28.9%	48.5%	32.0%
Winner	82.4% D	62.8% D	100.0% D

9

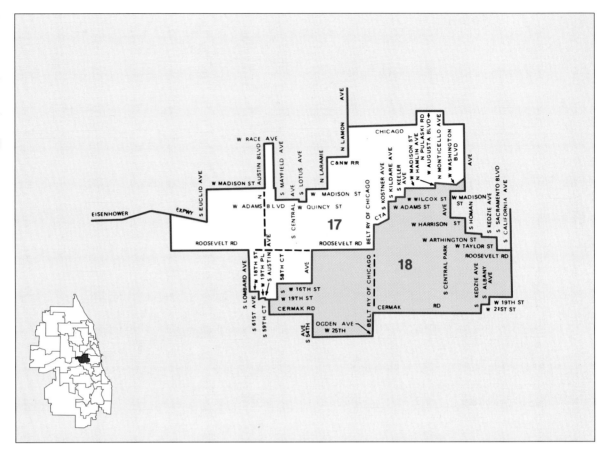

House District 17 covers half of West Garfield Park, three-tenths of Oak Park, Austin, and parts of Humboldt Park, Cicero, and East Garfield Park.

Most of North Lawndale and parts of Cicero, East Garfield Park, West Garfield Park, and South Lawndale are in House District 18.

Senate District 9 is one of the state's poorest districts. It ranks fifth lowest in median income, third lowest in median value of owner-occupied housing units, and fourth in the percentage of families falling below the poverty line. The district also ranks sixth in the proportion of population lacking a high school diploma.

	H.D. 17	H.D. 18	S.D. 9
Voting Age Population	55,886	57,989	113,875
White	33.6%	26.4%	29.9%
Black	63.6%	70.1%	66.9%
Hispanic	2.2%	3.5%	2.9%
Asian	.7%	.0%	.3%
Age (Total Population)	97,728	97,564	195,292
Under 6	11.6%	11.6%	11.6%
6 to 18	26.8%	27.8%	27.3%
65 and Over	6.6%	8.3%	7.4%
Education (Age 25 and over)	48,195	47,215	95,410
Less than 12 Years	43.4%	58.9%	51.0%
16 Years or More	9.2%	3.7%	6.5%
Urban Population	100.0%	100.0%	100.0%
Family Income (Total Families)	22,365	22,028	44,393
Median Income	$16,519	$12,253	$14,222
Below Poverty Level	9.5%	15.2%	12.3%
With Children Under 6	4.4%	5.1%	4.8%
With Children 6 to 17	7.5%	11.0%	9.2%
Headed by Females	5.8%	8.7%	7.3%
Industry (Total Employed)	31,013	28,825	59,838
Professional/Public Admin.	24.2%	20.7%	22.5%
Manufacturing	29.4%	35.2%	32.2%
Retail	15.2%	16.1%	15.6%
Transportation/Communication	10.0%	8.6%	9.3%
Finance/Insurance/Real Estate	5.7%	4.9%	5.3%
Other Service	7.4%	7.7%	7.5%
Housing Units (Total)	31,531	32,076	63,607
Median Value	$49,844	$38,006	$43,925
Owner Occupied	35.7%	25.6%	30.6%
Election Results			
1982 Turnout	45.3%	43.1%	44.0%
Winner	78.2% D	100.0% D	99.4% D
1984 Turnout	52.5%	48.4%	N E
Winner	66.5% D	82.7% D	N E
1986 Turnout	35.8%	35.2%	36.2%
Winner	78.7% D	82.0% D	80.9% D

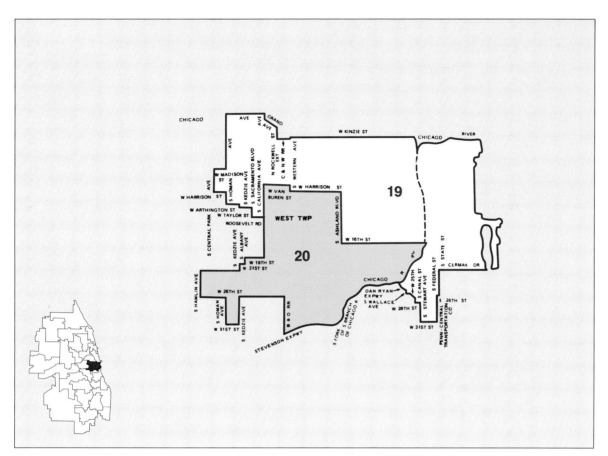

The Loop, the major portions of East Garfield Park, Near West Side, Near South Side, and Armour Square, and slices of Humboldt Park and North Lawndale are in House District 19.

The Lower West Side is in House District 20, along with parts of East Garfield Park, Near West Side, and North and South Lawndale.

Senate District 10 ranks second in the state in the percentage of families falling below the poverty level, second lowest in median income, and fourth lowest in median value of owner-occupied housing.

	H.D. 19	H.D. 20	S.D. 10
Voting Age Population	**56,109**	**74,401**	**130,510**
White	22.0%	35.9%	29.9%
Black	66.3%	9.5%	33.9%
Hispanic	3.7%	53.9%	32.3%
Asian	8.0%	.6%	3.8%
Age (Total Population)	**96,616**	**98,118**	**194,734**
Under 6	11.5%	14.4%	13.0%
6 to 18	25.7%	25.0%	25.3%
65 and Over	9.3%	6.5%	7.9%
Education (Age 25 and over)	**48,353**	**45,828**	**94,181**
Less than 12 Years	56.1%	75.0%	65.3%
16 Years or More	10.0%	4.9%	7.5%
Urban Population	**100.0%**	**100.0%**	**100.0%**
Family Income (Total Families)	**19,972**	**20,566**	**40,538**
Median Income	$9,329	$14,012	$11,763
Below Poverty Level	19.9%	12.5%	16.2%
With Children Under 6	8.3%	6.0%	7.1%
With Children 6 to 17	14.5%	7.6%	11.0%
Headed by Females	13.3%	3.8%	8.5%
Industry (Total Employed)	**25,855**	**33,319**	**59,174**
Professional/Public Admin.	33.2%	14.0%	22.4%
Manufacturing	23.5%	47.3%	36.9%
Retail	14.5%	11.4%	12.8%
Transportation/Communication	8.1%	6.3%	7.1%
Finance/Insurance/Real Estate	7.2%	4.3%	5.6%
Other Service	8.3%	7.1%	7.6%
Housing Units (Total)	**36,513**	**30,393**	**66,096**
Median Value	$32,390	$21,466	$26,928
Owner Occupied	15.9%	23.2%	19.2%
Election Results			
1982 Turnout	51.2%	19.7%	33.1%
Winner	100.0% D	67.4% D	100.0% D
1984 Turnout	44.6%	17.7%	29.4%
Winner	100.0% D	100.0% D	100.0% D
1986 Turnout	35.1%	13.6%	N E
Winner	85.5% D	87.4% D	N E

11th

Senate

DISTRICT

House District 21
House District 22

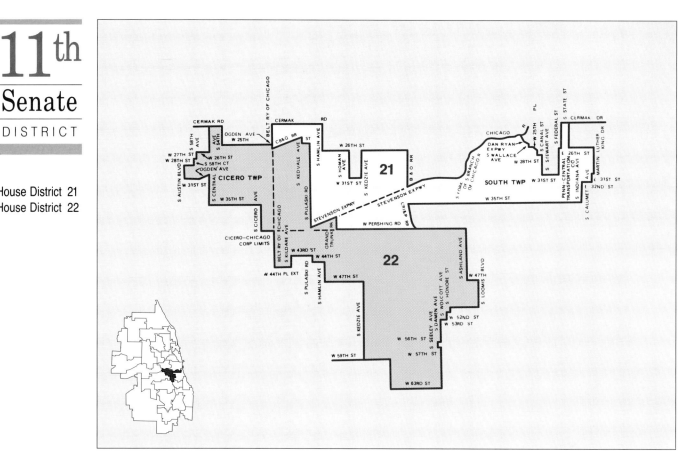

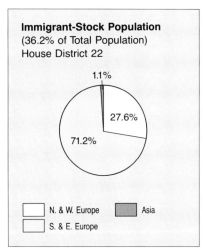

Immigrant-Stock Population
(36.2% of Total Population)
House District 22

1.1%

27.6%

71.2%

☐ N. & W. Europe ▨ Asia
☐ S. & E. Europe

Large sections of Bridgeport and McKinley Park and smaller ones of South Lawndale, Douglas, and Brighton Park make up most of House District 21.

The major part of House District 22 covers most of Gage Park and Brighton Park along with smaller portions of Archer Heights, West Englewood, Cicero, and New City.

	H.D. 21	H.D. 22	S.D. 11
Voting Age Population	74,709	76,306	151,015
White	59.2%	78.0%	68.7%
Black	17.6%	2.0%	9.7%
Hispanic	22.0%	19.8%	20.9%
Asian	1.3%	.2%	.7%
Age (Total Population)	96,305	95,805	192,110
Under 6	10.2%	9.6%	9.9%
6 to 18	21.1%	18.8%	19.9%
65 and Over	10.0%	13.2%	11.6%
Education (Age 25 and over)	51,947	57,536	109,483
Less than 12 Years	58.1%	58.7%	58.4%
16 Years or More	6.0%	5.4%	5.7%
Urban Population	100.0%	100.0%	100.0%
Family Income (Total Families)	21,511	24,207	45,718
Median Income	$17,544	$19,777	$18,770
Below Poverty Level	8.0%	4.7%	6.3%
With Children Under 6	4.4%	2.5%	3.4%
With Children 6 to 17	5.9%	3.0%	4.4%
Headed by Females	3.1%	1.2%	2.1%
Industry (Total Employed)	35,348	42,060	77,408
Professional/Public Admin.	19.7%	14.5%	16.9%
Manufacturing	30.7%	35.7%	33.4%
Retail	15.5%	15.4%	15.5%
Transportation/Communication	9.9%	10.0%	9.9%
Finance/Insurance/Real Estate	7.2%	7.1%	7.1%
Other Service	7.0%	6.4%	6.7%
Housing Units (Total)	32,910	37,101	70,011
Median Value	$29,201	$35,172	$32,187
Owner Occupied	34.0%	45.1%	39.9%
Election Results			
1982 Turnout	35.1%	32.1%	38.3%
Winner	100.0% D	100.0% D	84.9% D
1984 Turnout	34.9%	37.4%	N E
Winner	78.3% D	65.3% D	N E
1986 Turnout	28.2%	29.7%	28.7%
Winner	89.3% D	73.9% D	78.9% D

12

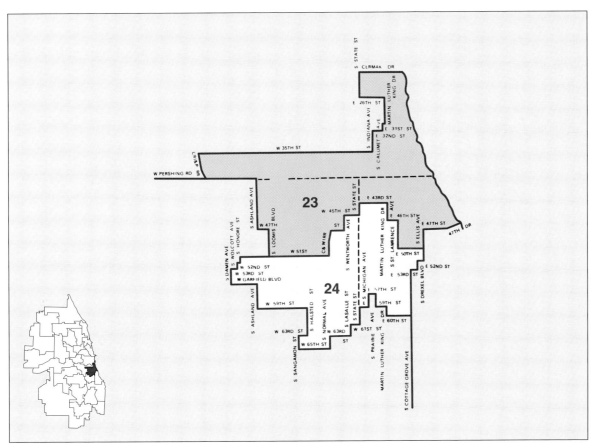

All of Oakland, most of Kenwood and Grand Boulevard, half of New City and McKinley Park, sizable segments of Bridgeport, Douglas, and Fuller Park, and smaller parts of Armour Square and Near South Side are in House District 23.

Most of Washington Park and Fuller Park, half of Englewood, four-tenths of Grand Boulevard, and small slices of Kenwood, Hyde Park, New City, and West Englewood make up House District 24.

Senate District 12 has the lowest median income in the state, as well as the lowest median value of owner-occupied housing and the highest percentage of families falling below the poverty level.

	H.D. 23	H.D. 24	S.D. 12
Voting Age Population	59,907	59,984	115,891
White	15.4%	6.7%	10.9%
Black	79.3%	88.1%	83.8%
Hispanic	4.6%	5.2%	4.9%
Asian	.7%	.0%	.3%
Age (Total Population)	97,036	97,662	194,698
Under 6	11.9%	12.4%	12.1%
6 to 18	27.1%	27.4%	27.3%
65 and Over	11.3%	9.8%	10.5%
Education (Age 25 and over)	47,865	47,422	95,287
Less than 12 Years	56.4%	64.1%	60.2%
16 Years or More	8.6%	3.2%	5.9%
Urban Population	100.0%	100.0%	100.0%
Family Income (Total Families)	20,529	20,079	40,608
Median Income	$8,480	$9,272	$8,778
Below Poverty Level	20.7%	22.2%	21.4%
With Children Under 6	7.8%	6.4%	7.1%
With Children 6 to 17	16.0%	14.3%	15.2%
Headed by Females	12.2%	13.2%	12.7%
Industry (Total Employed)	23,004	24,392	47,396
Professional/Public Admin.	36.3%	25.3%	30.7%
Manufacturing	19.8%	27.5%	23.8%
Retail	12.1%	14.2%	13.2%
Transportation/Communication	10.2%	10.2%	10.2%
Finance/Insurance/Real Estate	7.0%	5.4%	6.2%
Other Service	9.2%	10.6%	9.9%
Housing Units (Total)	37,845	34,427	72,272
Median Value	$23,415	$24,287	$23,851
Owner Occupied	11.1%	16.6%	13.7%
Election Results			
1982 Turnout	49.7%	46.8%	49.5%
Winner	100.0% D	100.0% D	100.0% D
1984 Turnout	50.3%	38.8%	N E
Winner	54.3% D	100.0% D	N E
1986 Turnout	33.5%	27.9%	31.4%
Winner	90.5% D	95.9% D	95.5% D

13

13th

Senate

DISTRICT

House District 25
House District 26

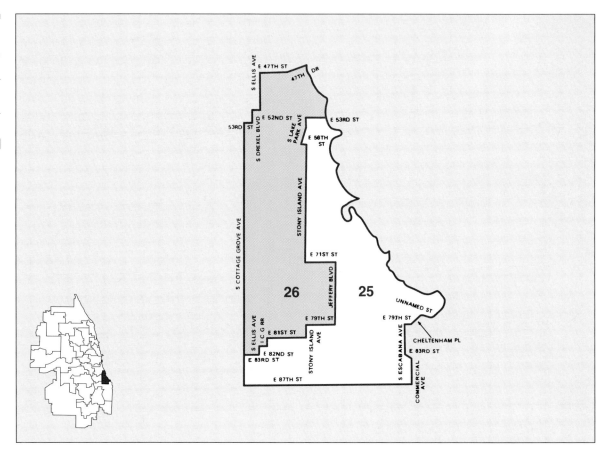

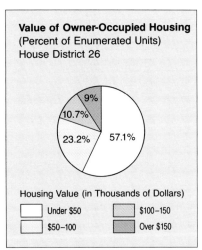

Value of Owner-Occupied Housing
(Percent of Enumerated Units)
House District 26

9%
10.7%
23.2%
57.1%

Housing Value (in Thousands of Dollars)

☐ Under $50	☐ $100–150
☐ $50–100	■ Over $150

House District 25 includes most of Avalon Park and South Shore and parts of Hyde Park, Woodlawn, Chatham, and South Chicago.

The major part of Hyde Park is in House District 26, along with half of Woodlawn, four-tenths of Kenwood and South Shore, and parts of Avalon Park, Chatham, and Greater Grand Crossing.

	H.D. 25	H.D. 26	S.D. 13
Voting Age Population	71,403	67,234	138,637
White	14.6%	22.8%	18.6%
Black	80.9%	74.3%	77.7%
Hispanic	4.0%	1.0%	2.6%
Asian	.5%	1.8%	1.1%
Age (Total Population)	97,490	96,914	194,404
Under 6	9.3%	8.8%	9.0%
6 to 18	20.6%	19.1%	19.9%
65 and Over	7.2%	9.2%	8.2%
Education (Age 25 and over)	56,692	57,046	113,738
Less than 12 Years	30.3%	31.1%	30.7%
16 Years or More	20.0%	25.6%	22.8%
Urban Population	100.0%	100.0%	100.0%
Family Income (Total Families)	23,171	21,926	45,097
Median Income	$19,418	$15,419	$17,465
Below Poverty Level	6.2%	9.3%	7.7%
With Children Under 6	3.9%	4.4%	4.1%
With Children 6 to 17	5.5%	7.2%	6.3%
Headed by Females	3.1%	4.5%	3.8%
Industry (Total Employed)	45,723	38,867	84,590
Professional/Public Admin.	37.2%	45.0%	40.8%
Manufacturing	17.3%	14.5%	16.0%
Retail	11.3%	11.3%	11.3%
Transportation/Communication	13.0%	9.0%	11.1%
Finance/Insurance/Real Estate	8.9%	6.8%	8.0%
Other Service	7.8%	9.1%	8.4%
Housing Units (Total)	41,007	42,327	83,334
Median Value	$37,919	$43,626	$40,773
Owner Occupied	28.6%	21.3%	24.9%
Election Results			
1982 Turnout	43.9%	44.1%	44.1%
Winner	96.0% D	100.0% D	100.0% D
1984 Turnout	47.4%	47.9%	47.9%
Winner	100.0% D	100.0% D	100.0% D
1986 Turnout	35.4%	35.3%	N E
Winner	95.6% D	95.9% D	N E

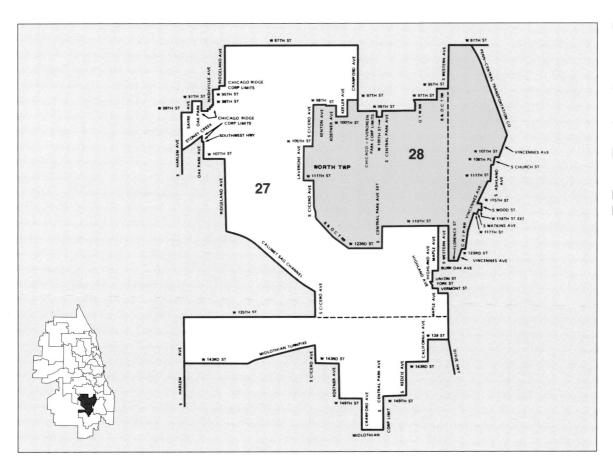

Parts of Bremen and Worth Townships make up House District 27.

All of Beverly and Mount Greenwood are in House District 28, along with half of Morgan Park and parts of Worth and Calumet Townships.

With 15.6 percent, House District 28 ranks second highest in Illinois in the proportion of its work force employed by local government.

	H.D. 27	H.D. 28	S.D. 14
Voting Age Population	**66,675**	**62,543**	**129,218**
White	89.5%	89.9%	89.7%
Black	7.9%	8.7%	8.3%
Hispanic	2.3%	1.3%	1.8%
Asian	.3%	.1%	.2%
Age (Total Population)	**97,144**	**96,749**	**193,893**
Under 6	8.5%	7.2%	7.8%
6 to 18	22.3%	20.3%	21.3%
65 and Over	10.1%	15.9%	13.0%
Education (Age 25 and over)	**55,031**	**60,211**	**115,242**
Less than 12 Years	33.6%	26.8%	30.0%
16 Years or More	10.6%	18.5%	14.7%
Urban Population	**100.0%**	**100.0%**	**100.0%**
Family Income (Total Families)	**24,855**	**25,250**	**50,105**
Median Income	$24,476	$26,552	$25,514
Below Poverty Level	2.3%	1.9%	2.1%
With Children Under 6	1.1%	.5%	.8%
With Children 6 to 17	2.3%	1.0%	1.6%
Headed by Females	.7%	.3%	.5%
Industry (Total Employed)	**45,054**	**43,505**	**88,559**
Professional/Public Admin.	19.9%	30.9%	25.3%
Manufacturing	23.8%	16.0%	20.0%
Retail	18.7%	16.3%	17.5%
Transportation/Communication	11.4%	9.7%	10.6%
Finance/Insurance/Real Estate	7.5%	9.9%	8.7%
Other Service	6.9%	6.9%	6.9%
Housing Units (Total)	**33,499**	**34,123**	**67,622**
Median Value	$57,821	$57,444	$57,633
Owner Occupied	68.4%	74.2%	71.4%
Election Results			
1982 Turnout	43.2%	63.7%	55.1%
Winner	56.1% D	68.3% D	62.9% D
1984 Turnout	50.5%	70.4%	N E
Winner	51.2% D	62.5% D	N E
1986 Turnout	35.8%	57.6%	46.7%
Winner	66.9% D	73.1% D	69.4% D

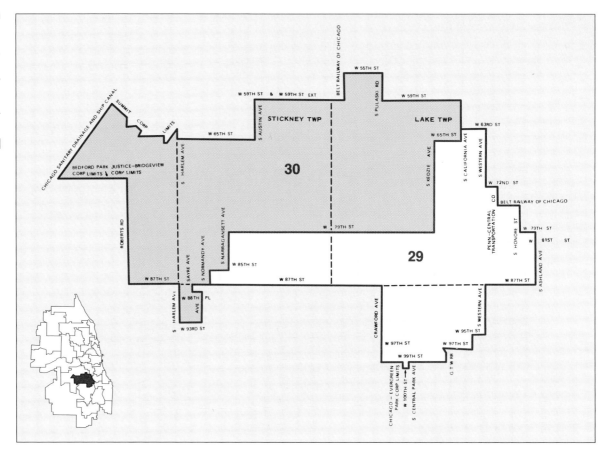

15th
Senate
DISTRICT

House District 29
House District 30

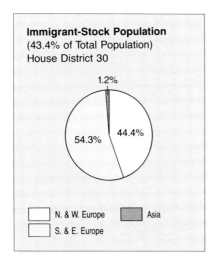

Immigrant-Stock Population
(43.4% of Total Population)
House District 30

1.2%

44.4%

54.3%

| | N. & W. Europe | | Asia |
| S. & E. Europe | | | |

Most of Ashburn is in House District 29, as is almost half of Chicago Lawn and slices of Auburn Gresham and Stickney and Worth Townships.

All of West Lawn and half of Clearing are in House District 30, along with smaller parts of West Elsden, Chicago Lawn, Ashburn, and the Cook County townships of Lyons, Stickney and Worth.

	H.D. 29	H.D. 30	S.D. 15
Voting Age Population	67,996	62,760	130,756
White	79.3%	96.1%	87.3%
Black	17.5%	.1%	9.1%
Hispanic	2.9%	3.7%	3.3%
Asian	.4%	.1%	.3%
Age (Total Population)	97,635	96,418	194,053
Under 6	7.1%	7.3%	7.2%
6 to 18	20.6%	19.8%	20.2%
65 and Over	13.4%	13.1%	13.3%
Education (Age 25 and over)	60,210	59,772	119,982
Less than 12 Years	36.5%	40.9%	38.7%
16 Years or More	10.7%	6.3%	8.5%
Urban Population	100.0%	100.0%	100.0%
Family Income (Total Families)	25,526	25,840	51,366
Median Income	$25,286	$24,919	$25,099
Below Poverty Level	2.2%	1.8%	2.0%
With Children Under 6	.6%	.7%	.6%
With Children 6 to 17	1.6%	1.5%	1.6%
Headed by Females	.4%	.2%	.3%
Industry (Total Employed)	47,323	44,169	91,492
Professional/Public Admin.	25.1%	19.0%	22.2%
Manufacturing	23.0%	27.2%	25.0%
Retail	17.0%	18.0%	17.5%
Transportation/Communication	11.6%	12.6%	12.1%
Finance/Insurance/Real Estate	7.1%	7.1%	7.1%
Other Service	6.2%	6.0%	6.1%
Housing Units (Total)	33,169	33,883	67,052
Median Value	$51,826	$51,417	$51,623
Owner Occupied	73.2%	73.3%	73.3%
Election Results			
1982 Turnout	54.6%	60.9%	59.3%
Winner	64.5% D	76.9% D	65.8% D
1984 Turnout	60.7%	65.4%	N E
Winner	59.6% D	67.6% D	N E
1986 Turnout	50.2%	56.6%	52.8%
Winner	64.1% D	78.7% D	72.8% D

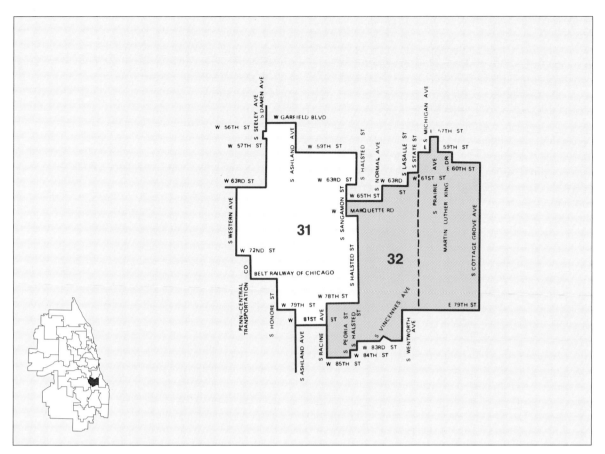

House District 31 includes most of West Englewood and parts of Chicago Lawn, Englewood, and Auburn Gresham.

Three-quarters of Greater Grand Crossing is in House District 32, along with portions of Washington Park, Woodlawn, Chatham, Englewood, and Auburn Gresham.

Senate District 16 ranks third in the state in the percentage of families falling below the poverty line. It is third lowest in median income and sixth lowest in median value of owner-occupied housing.

	H.D. 31	H.D. 32	S.D. 16
Voting Age Population	**52,328**	**59,118**	**111,446**
White	1.0%	.1%	.5%
Black	98.5%	99.7%	99.1%
Hispanic	.5%	.2%	.4%
Asian	.0%	.0%	.0%
Age (Total Population)	**96,096**	**96,677**	**192,773**
Under 6	11.5%	9.4%	10.4%
6 to 18	29.2%	22.3%	25.8%
65 and Over	5.3%	13.2%	9.3%
Education (Age 25 and over)	**45,040**	**55,702**	**100,742**
Less than 12 Years	50.7%	46.9%	48.6%
16 Years or More	4.1%	6.3%	5.3%
Urban Population	**100.0%**	**100.0%**	**100.0%**
Family Income (Total Families)	**21,359**	**22,965**	**44,324**
Median Income	$14,327	$12,574	$13,462
Below Poverty Level	13.0%	12.8%	12.9%
With Children Under 6	3.9%	4.5%	4.2%
With Children 6 to 17	9.3%	8.7%	9.0%
Headed by Females	7.6%	6.1%	6.8%
Industry (Total Employed)	**28,966**	**31,087**	**60,053**
Professional/Public Admin.	26.7%	31.0%	28.9%
Manufacturing	26.8%	21.3%	24.0%
Retail	13.0%	13.1%	13.0%
Transportation/Communication	13.0%	13.1%	13.0%
Finance/Insurance/Real Estate	5.9%	6.7%	6.3%
Other Service	7.7%	9.7%	8.8%
Housing Units (Total)	**27,947**	**37,027**	**64,974**
Median Value	$29,090	$32,189	$30,639
Owner Occupied	44.6%	25.3%	33.3%
Election Results			
1982 Turnout	58.2%	60.7%	60.0%
Winner	100.0% D	97.2% D	100.0% D
1984 Turnout	61.7%	57.4%	60.6%
Winner	100.0% D	100.0% D	100.0% D
1986 Turnout	40.9%	40.7%	41.1%
Winner	97.1% D	95.9% D	100.0% D

17th
Senate
DISTRICT

House District 33
House District 34

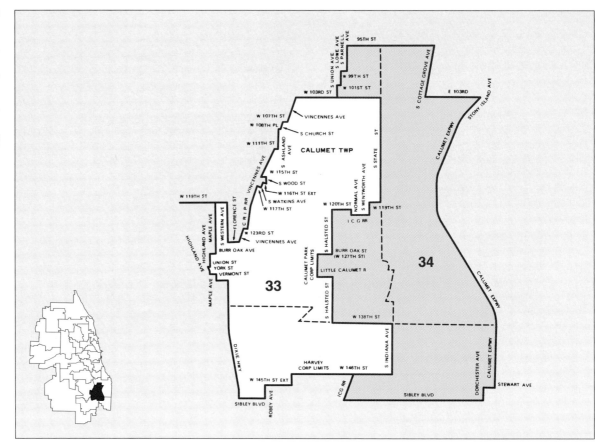

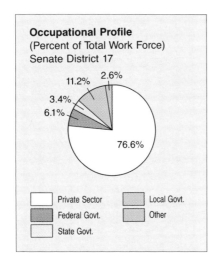

Occupational Profile
(Percent of Total Work Force)
Senate District 17

2.6%
11.2%
3.4%
6.1%
76.6%

Private Sector	Local Govt.
Federal Govt.	Other
State Govt.	

Half of Morgan Park, almost half of West Pullman, and parts of the communities of Roseland and Washington Heights and the townships of Calumet, Worth, and Thornton make up House District 33.

All of Riverdale, 60 percent of both Pullman and West Pullman, 50 percent of Roseland, and slices of Washington Heights and the townships of Calumet and Thornton are in House District 34.

	H.D. 33	H.D. 34	S.D. 17
Voting Age Population	**61,811**	**60,783**	**122,594**
White	36.4%	27.3%	31.9%
Black	60.3%	69.4%	64.8%
Hispanic	3.2%	3.2%	3.2%
Asian	.1%	.1%	.1%
Age (Total Population)	**96,424**	**96,849**	**193,273**
Under 6	9.4%	10.5%	10.0%
6 to 18	25.4%	27.5%	26.4%
65 and Over	8.6%	5.7%	7.1%
Education (Age 25 and over)	**51,134**	**49,129**	**100,263**
Less than 12 Years	39.2%	37.3%	38.2%
16 Years or More	7.7%	8.6%	8.1%
Urban Population	**100.0%**	**100.0%**	**100.0%**
Family Income (Total Families)	**22,738**	**23,313**	**46,051**
Median Income	$21,403	$21,229	$21,317
Below Poverty Level	5.0%	7.2%	6.1%
With Children Under 6	1.1%	2.4%	1.8%
With Children 6 to 17	5.0%	6.0%	5.5%
Headed by Females	1.9%	4.0%	2.9%
Industry (Total Employed)	**37,639**	**37,476**	**75,115**
Professional/Public Admin.	24.8%	25.7%	25.2%
Manufacturing	24.6%	25.6%	25.1%
Retail	14.9%	13.1%	14.0%
Transportation/Communication	12.8%	13.9%	13.3%
Finance/Insurance/Real Estate	8.2%	7.5%	7.8%
Other Service	7.5%	7.1%	7.3%
Housing Units (Total)	**30,506**	**29,475**	**59,981**
Median Value	$39,215	$40,858	$40,036
Owner Occupied	64.9%	61.8%	63.4%
Election Results			
1982 Turnout	51.0%	49.5%	51.6%
Winner	82.4% D	75.2% D	84.2% D
1984 Turnout	57.3%	55.0%	N E
Winner	81.1% D	83.3% D	N E
1986 Turnout	40.7%	38.0%	39.9%
Winner	82.8% D	84.6% D	83.9% D

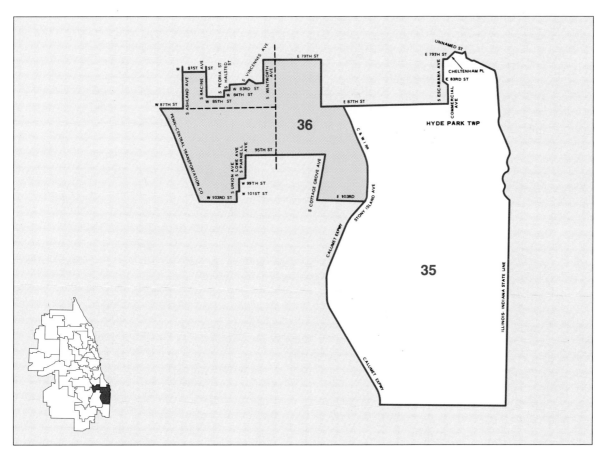

House District 35
House District 36

House District 35 contains all of Calumet Heights, South Deering, East Side, and Hegewich, along with 70 percent of South Chicago.

Burnside and major portions of Chatham and Washington Heights, as well as smaller parts of Auburn Gresham, Pullman, and Roseland are in House District 36.

House District 36 has a higher proportion of its work force employed by the federal government (9.8%) and by local government (17.0%) than any other district in Illinois.

	H.D. 35	H.D. 36	S.D. 18
Voting Age Population	**70,887**	**63,052**	**133,939**
White	49.4%	1.3%	26.8%
Black	30.9%	98.4%	62.7%
Hispanic	19.7%	.3%	10.5%
Asian	.1%	.0%	.1%
Age (Total Population)	**96,064**	**95,936**	**192,000**
Under 6	8.7%	7.7%	8.2%
6 to 18	23.9%	23.0%	23.4%
65 and Over	8.7%	8.4%	8.5%
Education (Age 25 and over)	**53,744**	**55,550**	**109,294**
Less than 12 Years	46.6%	33.4%	39.9%
16 Years or More	8.0%	11.8%	9.9%
Urban Population	**100.0%**	**100.0%**	**100.0%**
Family Income (Total Families)	**24,051**	**23,643**	**47,694**
Median Income	$23,044	$21,714	$22,381
Below Poverty Level	4.1%	4.3%	4.2%
With Children Under 6	1.7%	1.4%	1.6%
With Children 6 to 17	3.6%	4.0%	3.8%
Headed by Females	1.1%	1.8%	1.4%
Industry (Total Employed)	**39,458**	**40,852**	**80,310**
Professional/Public Admin.	24.7%	32.4%	28.6%
Manufacturing	33.8%	21.0%	27.3%
Retail	12.3%	12.8%	12.5%
Transportation/Communication	10.2%	15.3%	12.8%
Finance/Insurance/Real Estate	6.4%	7.1%	6.8%
Other Service	5.7%	6.3%	6.0%
Housing Units (Total)	**32,149**	**31,585**	**63,734**
Median Value	$37,609	$39,523	$38,566
Owner Occupied	60.2%	57.8%	59.0%
Election Results			
1982 Turnout	47.1%	47.1%	50.8%
Winner	88.5% D	97.1% D	100.0% D
1984 Turnout	43.5%	63.3%	N E
Winner	100.0% D	100.0% D	N E
1986 Turnout	40.4%	50.1%	45.0%
Winner	89.8% D	97.5% D	91.3% D

19

19th Senate DISTRICT

House District 37
House District 38

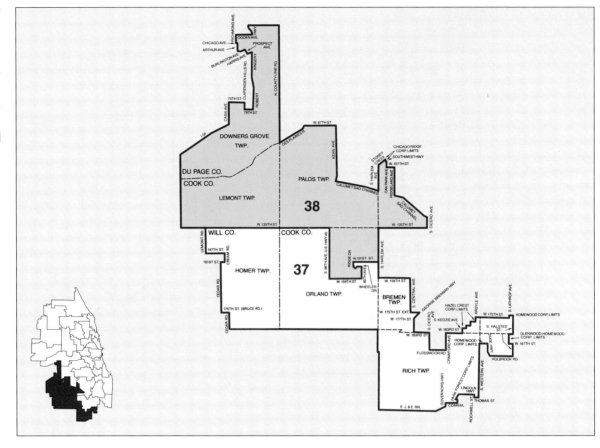

Senate District 19 is a suburban Cook County district, although it also contains small parts of Du-Page and Will Counties.

The district ranks fourth in the state in median income and sixth in median value of owner-occupied housing, with nearly a third of the housing valued over $100,000.

	H.D. 37	H.D. 38	S.D. 19
Voting Age Population	**69,717**	**56,915**	**126,632**
White	94.9%	96.7%	95.7%
Black	2.9%	.5%	1.8%
Hispanic	1.1%	1.0%	1.1%
Asian	1.1%	1.8%	1.4%
Age (Total Population)	**96,317**	**93,129**	**189,446**
Under 6	9.5%	7.7%	8.6%
6 to 18	23.3%	23.3%	23.3%
65 and Over	7.2%	8.2%	7.7%
Education (Age 25 and over)	**55,535**	**54,645**	**110,180**
Less than 12 Years	20.4%	18.8%	19.6%
16 Years or More	26.0%	25.1%	25.5%
Urban Population	**86.2%**	**93.2%**	**89.6%**
Family Income (Total Families)	**25,735**	**24,587**	**50,322**
Median Income	$30,189	$31,848	$30,875
Below Poverty Level	1.3%	1.3%	1.3%
With Children Under 6	.4%	.4%	.4%
With Children 6 to 17	1.2%	.7%	1.0%
Headed by Females	.3%	.3%	.3%
Industry (Total Employed)	**50,573**	**43,403**	**93,976**
Professional/Public Admin.	23.0%	22.0%	22.5%
Manufacturing	21.7%	21.8%	21.8%
Retail	19.0%	16.9%	18.0%
Transportation/Communication	9.8%	8.4%	9.2%
Finance/Insurance/Real Estate	8.6%	7.6%	8.2%
Other Service	6.9%	9.8%	8.3%
Housing Units (Total)	**32,306**	**31,778**	**64,084**
Median Value	$73,497	$91,541	$82,519
Owner Occupied	79.1%	73.5%	76.3%
Election Results			
1982 Turnout	41.3%	53.5%	48.3%
Winner	60.0% R	60.3% R	68.8% R
1984 Turnout	58.1%	61.7%	65.8%
Winner	71.2% R	100.0% R	68.4% R
1986 Turnout	33.0%	50.2%	N E
Winner	100.0% R	77.5% R	N E

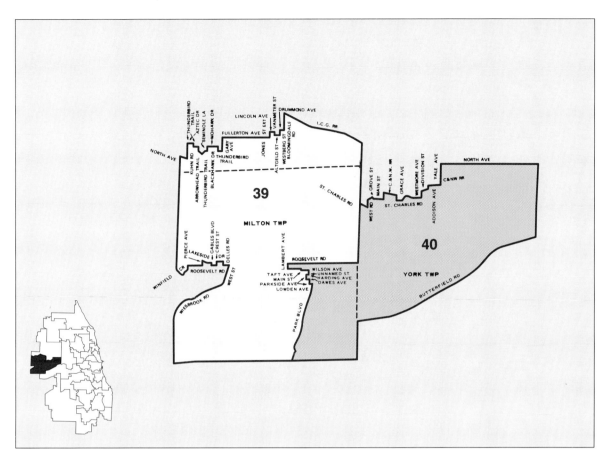

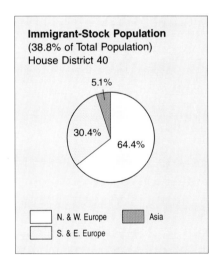

Immigrant-Stock Population
(38.8% of Total Population)
House District 40

5.1%

30.4%   64.4%

☐ N. & W. Europe   ▨ Asia
☐ S. & E. Europe

Senate District 20 ranks sixth in Illinois in median income, and it is in the top quarter in median value of owner-occupied housing, with almost nine-tenths of its units valued between $50,000 and $150,000.

	H.D. 39	H.D. 40	S.D. 20
Voting Age Population	**72,088**	**68,473**	**140,561**
White	95.0%	97.0%	96.0%
Black	1.6%	.6%	1.1%
Hispanic	1.5%	1.1%	1.3%
Asian	1.9%	1.3%	1.6%
Age (Total Population)	**97,307**	**97,234**	**194,541**
Under 6	8.8%	6.9%	7.9%
6 to 18	23.0%	21.4%	22.2%
65 and Over	6.9%	9.2%	8.1%
Education (Age 25 and over)	**54,892**	**59,097**	**113,989**
Less than 12 Years	14.8%	17.8%	16.3%
16 Years or More	38.3%	28.3%	33.1%
Urban Population	**100.0%**	**100.0%**	**100.0%**
Family Income (Total Families)	**24,913**	**25,983**	**50,896**
Median Income	$30,509	$29,977	$30,247
Below Poverty Level	1.1%	1.1%	1.1%
With Children Under 6	.7%	.4%	.5%
With Children 6 to 17	1.0%	.5%	.8%
Headed by Females	.3%	.2%	.2%
Industry (Total Employed)	**54,597**	**53,268**	**107,865**
Professional/Public Admin.	24.9%	23.4%	24.2%
Manufacturing	21.9%	21.4%	21.6%
Retail	17.0%	18.6%	17.8%
Transportation/Communication	7.7%	8.5%	8.1%
Finance/Insurance/Real Estate	7.5%	7.3%	7.4%
Other Service	9.9%	8.9%	9.4%
Housing Units (Total)	**34,387**	**34,933**	**69,320**
Median Value	$77,932	$72,514	$75,223
Owner Occupied	66.4%	74.7%	70.6%
Election Results			
1982 Turnout	38.6%	47.6%	43.0%
Winner	72.6% R	66.2% R	69.8% R
1984 Turnout	55.8%	60.9%	N E
Winner	76.2% R	71.3% R	N E
1986 Turnout	32.1%	41.7%	39.6%
Winner	100.0% R	70.6% R	71.3% R

21

21st

Senate

DISTRICT

House District 41
House District 42

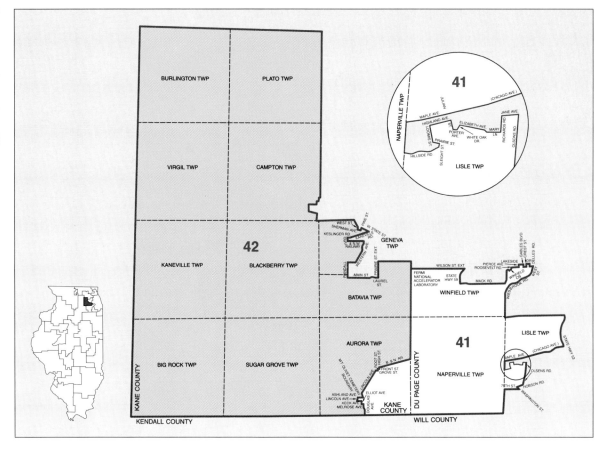

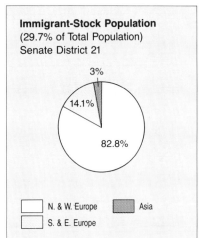

Immigrant-Stock Population
(29.7% of Total Population)
Senate District 21

3%
14.1%
82.8%

N. & W. Europe — Asia
S. & E. Europe

	H.D. 41	H.D. 42	S.D. 21
Voting Age Population	**65,608**	**65,853**	**131,461**
White	85.5%	90.4%	88.1%
Black	4.2%	4.2%	4.2%
Hispanic	9.2%	5.0%	7.1%
Asian	.8%	.4%	.6%
Age (Total Population)	**96,444**	**96,620**	**193,064**
Under 6	10.5%	10.0%	10.3%
6 to 18	23.0%	23.0%	23.0%
65 and Over	7.0%	8.4%	7.7%
Education (Age 25 and over)	**52,634**	**53,816**	**106,450**
Less than 12 Years	25.6%	25.8%	25.7%
16 Years or More	27.5%	18.2%	22.8%
Urban Population	**98.1%**	**76.1%**	**87.1%**
Family Income (Total Families)	**24,529**	**24,851**	**49,380**
Median Income	$27,993	$26,191	$27,057
Below Poverty Level	1.9%	1.8%	1.8%
With Children Under 6	1.1%	.9%	1.0%
With Children 6 to 17	1.4%	1.4%	1.4%
Headed by Females	.8%	.8%	.8%
Industry (Total Employed)	**47,269**	**46,944**	**94,213**
Professional/Public Admin.	19.7%	22.2%	20.9%
Manufacturing	31.0%	31.5%	31.2%
Retail	15.6%	13.7%	14.7%
Transportation/Communication	6.7%	6.8%	6.8%
Finance/Insurance/Real Estate	7.2%	6.4%	6.8%
Other Service	10.1%	7.0%	8.6%
Housing Units (Total)	**33,859**	**34,373**	**68,232**
Median Value	$69,902	$66,470	$68,186
Owner Occupied	69.2%	64.2%	66.7%
Election Results			
1982 Turnout	40.6%	39.3%	39.5%
Winner	55.9% R	67.3% R	61.5% R
1984 Turnout	45.0%	42.1%	N E
Winner	100.0% R	100.0% R	N E
1986 Turnout	31.9%	35.1%	30.1%
Winner	100.0% R	69.8% R	100.0% R

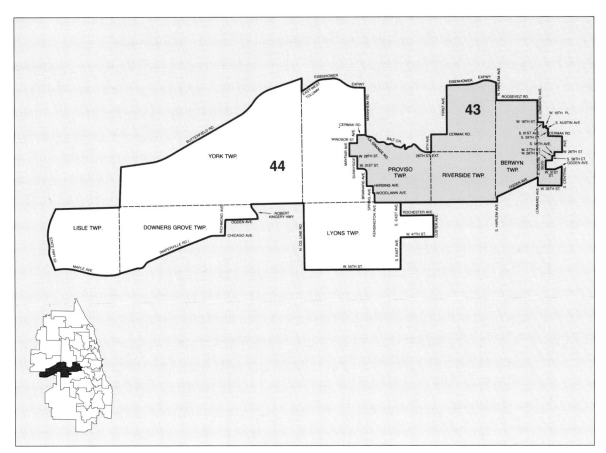

House District 43 is in Cook County, covering Riverside Township, most of Berwyn, and small sections of Cicero and Proviso Townships.

House District 44 includes parts of Lyons and Proviso Townships in Cook County and sections of three townships in DuPage County.

	H.D. 43	H.D. 44	S.D. 22
Voting Age Population	**69,902**	**63,278**	**133,180**
White	97.5%	96.0%	96.8%
Black	.2%	1.4%	.8%
Hispanic	1.7%	1.0%	1.4%
Asian	.6%	1.6%	1.0%
Age (Total Population)	**97,631**	**101,152**	**198,783**
Under 6	5.5%	6.6%	6.1%
6 to 18	15.3%	20.0%	17.7%
65 and Over	20.2%	12.2%	16.1%
Education (Age 25 and over)	**68,172**	**64,683**	**132,855**
Less than 12 Years	36.3%	16.0%	26.4%
16 Years or More	16.2%	30.4%	23.1%
Urban Population	**100.0%**	**100.0%**	**100.0%**
Family Income (Total Families)	**27,221**	**27,815**	**55,036**
Median Income	$25,168	$32,310	$28,231
Below Poverty Level	1.7%	.7%	1.2%
With Children Under 6	.5%	.2%	.4%
With Children 6 to 17	1.1%	.8%	.9%
Headed by Females	.1%	.1%	.1%
Industry (Total Employed)	**48,643**	**47,841**	**96,484**
Professional/Public Admin.	21.3%	24.7%	23.0%
Manufacturing	25.9%	22.7%	24.3%
Retail	17.9%	16.7%	17.3%
Transportation/Communication	8.6%	7.8%	8.2%
Finance/Insurance/Real Estate	8.7%	8.7%	8.7%
Other Service	7.2%	9.4%	8.3%
Housing Units (Total)	**41,631**	**37,085**	**78,716**
Median Value	$63,700	$83,157	$73,428
Owner Occupied	61.1%	75.5%	67.9%
Election Results			
1982 Turnout	48.9%	55.0%	52.9%
Winner	66.9% R	66.5% R	62.9% R
1984 Turnout	63.2%	73.6%	69.0%
Winner	63.4% R	71.8% R	74.4% R
1986 Turnout	45.5%	49.6%	N E
Winner	63.9% R	71.0% R	N E

23rd
Senate
DISTRICT

House District 45
House District 46

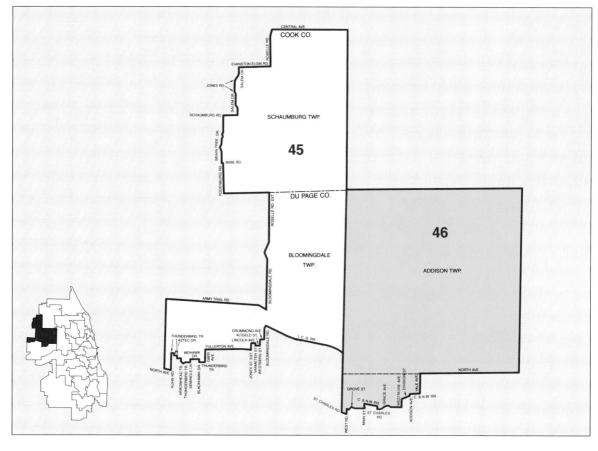

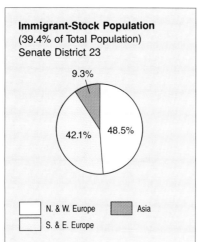

Immigrant-Stock Population
(39.4% of Total Population)
Senate District 23

9.3%

42.1%   48.5%

N. & W. Europe   ☐ Asia
S. & E. Europe

	H.D. 45	H.D. 46	S.D. 23
Voting Age Population	**64,801**	**66,305**	**131,106**
White	92.2%	93.5%	92.9%
Black	1.1%	.1%	.6%
Hispanic	2.6%	4.5%	3.5%
Asian	4.1%	1.9%	3.0%
Age (Total Population)	**96,269**	**97,575**	**193,844**
Under 6	10.6%	8.4%	9.5%
6 to 18	22.3%	23.4%	22.9%
65 and Over	4.3%	6.8%	5.6%
Education (Age 25 and over)	**53,671**	**55,555**	**109,226**
Less than 12 Years	15.8%	28.5%	22.3%
16 Years or More	25.7%	14.7%	20.1%
Urban Population	**100.0%**	**100.0%**	**100.0%**
Family Income (Total Families)	**24,834**	**25,499**	**50,333**
Median Income	$29,213	$28,197	$28,725
Below Poverty Level	1.1%	1.0%	1.0%
With Children Under 6	.7%	.7%	.7%
With Children 6 to 17	.9%	1.0%	.9%
Headed by Females	.1%	.1%	.1%
Industry (Total Employed)	**51,228**	**51,123**	**102,351**
Professional/Public Admin.	16.8%	13.7%	15.2%
Manufacturing	27.4%	31.0%	29.2%
Retail	16.2%	18.7%	17.5%
Transportation/Communication	9.7%	9.1%	9.4%
Finance/Insurance/Real Estate	7.8%	5.1%	6.5%
Other Service	8.0%	8.1%	8.0%
Housing Units (Total)	**35,601**	**32,574**	**68,175**
Median Value	$81,069	$71,338	$76,203
Owner Occupied	64.3%	71.4%	67.7%
Election Results			
1982 Turnout	31.7%	37.5%	34.7%
Winner	68.3% R	58.0% R	64.1% R
1984 Turnout	38.6%	38.8%	N E
Winner	100.0% R	100.0% R	N E
1986 Turnout	28.9%	30.4%	29.5%
Winner	100.0% R	100.0% R	100.0% R

24

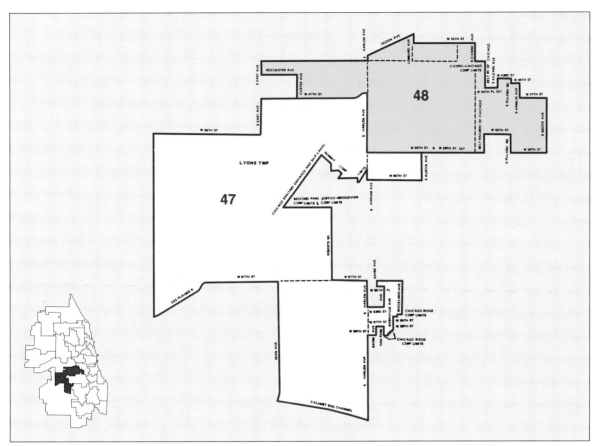

House District 47 includes half of Clearing in Chicago, half of Lyons Township, three-tenths of Palos Township, and small parts of Worth and Stickney Townships in Cook County.

House District 48 covers Garfield Ridge, most of Archer Heights and West Elsden, and small sections of Brighton Park and Gage Park, all in Chicago, and also parts of Berwyn, Cicero, Lyons, Stickney, and Lake Townships in Cook County.

	H.D. 47	H.D. 48	S.D. 24
Voting Age Population	66,421	66,826	133,245
White	92.8%	93.3%	93.1%
Black	3.0%	3.3%	3.2%
Hispanic	3.6%	3.0%	3.3%
Asian	.5%	.3%	.4%
Age (Total Population)	96,349	97,325	193,674
Under 6	8.1%	5.9%	7.0%
6 to 18	20.0%	17.7%	18.9%
65 and Over	8.3%	14.1%	11.2%
Education (Age 25 and over)	57,449	63,820	121,269
Less than 12 Years	32.4%	43.7%	38.3%
16 Years or More	12.6%	6.3%	9.3%
Urban Population	99.5%	100.0%	99.7%
Family Income (Total Families)	25,916	27,464	53,380
Median Income	$26,566	$24,092	$25,322
Below Poverty Level	2.0%	2.9%	2.5%
With Children Under 6	.8%	.4%	.6%
With Children 6 to 17	1.3%	1.4%	1.3%
Headed by Females	.6%	.5%	.6%
Industry (Total Employed)	47,367	44,649	92,016
Professional/Public Admin.	18.3%	17.9%	18.1%
Manufacturing	28.6%	30.1%	29.4%
Retail	16.9%	16.3%	16.6%
Transportation/Communication	10.8%	10.9%	10.8%
Finance/Insurance/Real Estate	6.6%	7.3%	6.9%
Other Service	7.1%	6.8%	7.0%
Housing Units (Total)	35,984	35,766	71,750
Median Value	$68,680	$53,630	$61,155
Owner Occupied	64.9%	74.0%	69.4%
Election Results			
1982 Turnout	42.1%	58.5%	53.1%
Winner	66.1% D	73.5% D	52.4% D
1984 Turnout	50.3%	62.5%	N E
Winner	54.2% D	59.5% D	N E
1986 Turnout	40.3%	55.3%	48.6%
Winner	50.4% D	57.2% D	54.7% R

25

25th
Senate
DISTRICT

House District 49
House District 50

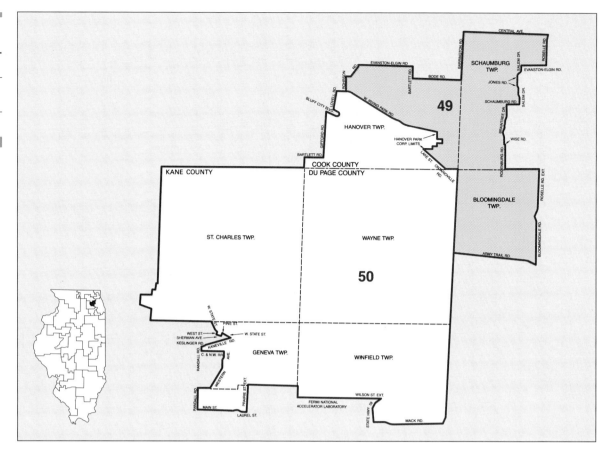

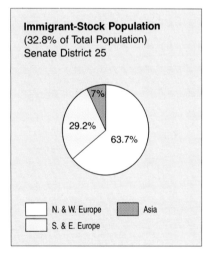

Immigrant-Stock Population
(32.8% of Total Population)
Senate District 25

7%
29.2%
63.7%

| | N. & W. Europe | | Asia |
| | S. & E. Europe | |

Senate District 25, which contains parts of Cook, DuPage, and Kane Counties, has a lower proportion of its population over sixty-five years of age than any other district in Illinois. It also ranks in the top third of the state's senate districts in percentage of college graduates.

	H.D. 49	H.D. 50	S.D. 25
Voting Age Population	**57,976**	**58,177**	**116,153**
White	93.4%	94.0%	93.7%
Black	.7%	.8%	.8%
Hispanic	3.3%	3.9%	3.6%
Asian	2.6%	1.3%	1.9%
Age (Total Population)	**97,163**	**96,692**	**193,855**
Under 6	11.5%	11.0%	11.2%
6 to 18	25.5%	22.7%	24.1%
65 and Over	2.6%	6.5%	4.5%
Education (Age 25 and over)	**51,528**	**53,306**	**104,834**
Less than 12 Years	16.0%	19.8%	17.9%
16 Years or More	19.7%	23.5%	21.6%
Urban Population	**99.9%**	**86.8%**	**93.4%**
Family Income (Total Families)	**25,013**	**25,223**	**50,236**
Median Income	$28,204	$27,843	$28,036
Below Poverty Level	1.0%	.9%	.9%
With Children Under 6	.5%	.6%	.5%
With Children 6 to 17	1.1%	.6%	.9%
Headed by Females	.3%	.2%	.2%
Industry (Total Employed)	**46,079**	**45,929**	**92,008**
Professional/Public Admin.	15.6%	20.3%	17.9%
Manufacturing	28.3%	28.9%	28.6%
Retail	17.9%	15.5%	16.7%
Transportation/Communication	10.5%	7.1%	8.8%
Finance/Insurance/Real Estate	7.1%	6.7%	6.9%
Other Service	7.4%	8.7%	8.0%
Housing Units (Total)	**32,264**	**33,514**	**65,778**
Median Value	$71,091	$73,847	$72,469
Owner Occupied	73.9%	72.7%	73.3%
Election Results			
1982 Turnout	33.2%	46.5%	40.0%
Winner	62.6% R	61.6% R	62.4% R
1984 Turnout	54.1%	57.7%	61.6%
Winner	68.0% R	100.0% R	74.8% R
1986 Turnout	31.6%	44.0%	N E
Winner	69.3% R	73.4% R	N E

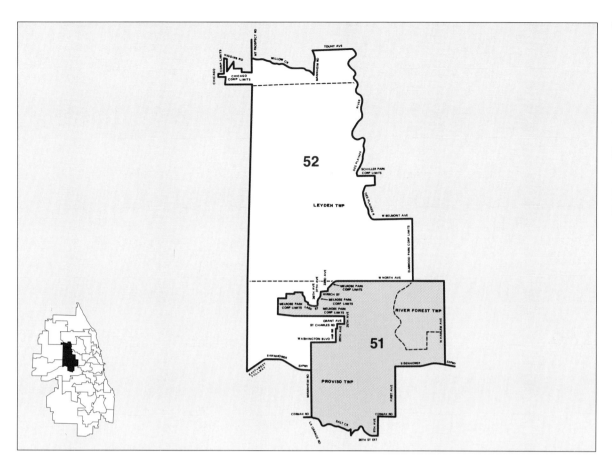

26th Senate DISTRICT

House District 51
House District 52

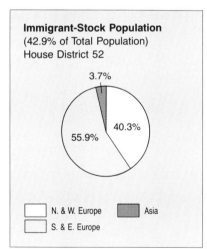

Immigrant-Stock Population
(42.9% of Total Population)
House District 52

3.7%

40.3%

55.9%

☐ N. & W. Europe   ■ Asia
☐ S. & E. Europe

The Chicago community of River Forest is in House District 51, along with a third of Proviso Township.

House District 52 includes half of O'Hare, most of Leyden Township, and smaller sections of Proviso and Maine Townships.

	H.D. 51	H.D. 52	S.D. 26
Voting Age Population	**70,258**	**71,970**	**142,228**
White	67.4%	90.9%	79.3%
Black	26.2%	1.8%	13.8%
Hispanic	5.3%	6.1%	5.7%
Asian	1.1%	1.1%	1.1%
Age (Total Population)	**96,881**	**95,811**	**192,692**
Under 6	8.0%	7.4%	7.7%
6 to 18	19.6%	19.3%	19.5%
65 and Over	11.9%	9.9%	10.9%
Education (Age 25 and over)	**58,855**	**58,403**	**117,258**
Less than 12 Years	32.4%	38.5%	35.4%
16 Years or More	16.5%	7.7%	12.1%
Urban Population	**100.0%**	**100.0%**	**100.0%**
Family Income (Total Families)	**24,465**	**25,649**	**50,114**
Median Income	$24,559	$25,589	$25,129
Below Poverty Level	3.1%	1.7%	2.4%
With Children Under 6	1.2%	.5%	.8%
With Children 6 to 17	1.8%	1.0%	1.4%
Headed by Females	1.0%	.4%	.7%
Industry (Total Employed)	**46,368**	**50,047**	**96,415**
Professional/Public Admin.	25.3%	14.1%	19.5%
Manufacturing	27.9%	36.3%	32.3%
Retail	14.7%	16.3%	15.6%
Transportation/Communication	10.6%	9.9%	10.3%
Finance/Insurance/Real Estate	6.5%	4.2%	5.3%
Other Service	6.0%	6.8%	6.4%
Housing Units (Total)	**35,535**	**35,626**	**71,161**
Median Value	$61,068	$63,034	$62,051
Owner Occupied	60.1%	66.2%	63.1%
Election Results			
1982 Turnout	42.9%	39.3%	43.6%
Winner	64.1% D	52.3% D	64.2% D
1984 Turnout	48.9%	45.5%	N E
Winner	64.8% D	56.8% R	N E
1986 Turnout	34.3%	32.9%	34.2%
Winner	71.9% D	53.8% R	71.3% D

27

27th
Senate
DISTRICT

House District 53
House District 54

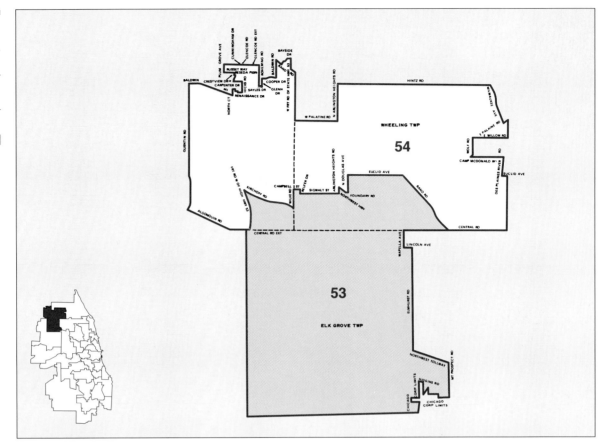

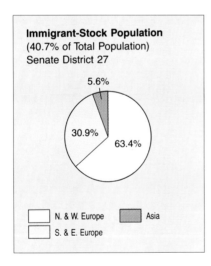

Immigrant-Stock Population
(40.7% of Total Population)
Senate District 27

5.6%

30.9%

63.4%

	N. & W. Europe	Asia
	S. & E. Europe	

Senate District 27, in Cook County, ranks fifth in the state in both median income and median value of owner-occupied housing. Over nine-tenths of its housing units are valued between $50,000 and $100,000.

	H.D. 53	H.D. 54	S.D. 27
Voting Age Population	68,228	72,007	140,235
White	94.7%	96.1%	95.4%
Black	.6%	.5%	.5%
Hispanic	2.5%	2.2%	2.3%
Asian	2.2%	1.3%	1.7%
Age (Total Population)	96,864	96,754	193,618
Under 6	6.9%	7.1%	7.0%
6 to 18	21.5%	23.0%	22.2%
65 and Over	6.6%	6.9%	6.8%
Education (Age 25 and over)	57,615	56,934	114,549
Less than 12 Years	17.6%	16.8%	17.2%
16 Years or More	24.4%	29.6%	27.0%
Urban Population	100.0%	100.0%	100.0%
Family Income (Total Families)	25,571	25,283	50,854
Median Income	$29,686	$31,277	$30,525
Below Poverty Level	.8%	1.0%	.9%
With Children Under 6	.5%	.4%	.5%
With Children 6 to 17	.8%	.7%	.7%
Headed by Females	.0%	.2%	.1%
Industry (Total Employed)	54,373	55,097	109,470
Professional/Public Admin.	16.9%	19.2%	18.0%
Manufacturing	27.3%	25.4%	26.3%
Retail	17.1%	16.6%	16.9%
Transportation/Communication	10.2%	7.5%	8.8%
Finance/Insurance/Real Estate	7.0%	9.4%	8.2%
Other Service	7.9%	9.1%	8.5%
Housing Units (Total)	36,999	35,041	72,040
Median Value	$83,442	$90,848	$87,145
Owner Occupied	62.7%	68.1%	65.3%
Election Results			
1982 Turnout	37.4%	38.0%	39.6%
Winner	64.5% R	70.1% R	74.1% R
1984 Turnout	38.0%	50.4%	N E
Winner	100.0% R	74.4% R	N E
1986 Turnout	31.8%	29.8%	29.9%
Winner	73.4% R	100.0% R	100.0% R

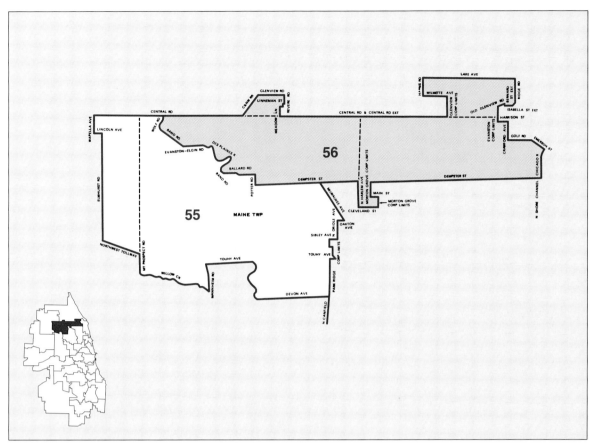

House District 55
House District 56

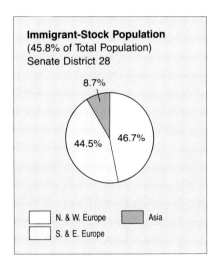

Immigrant-Stock Population
(45.8% of Total Population)
Senate District 28

8.7%

46.7%

44.5%

N. & W. Europe   Asia

S. & E. Europe

Senate District 28 ranks third in Illinois in median income and fourth in median value of owner-occupied housing.

	H.D. 55	H.D. 56	S.D. 28
Voting Age Population	**68,728**	**72,293**	**141,021**
White	96.4%	92.9%	94.6%
Black	.0%	.8%	.4%
Hispanic	2.2%	1.9%	2.1%
Asian	1.4%	4.3%	2.9%
Age (Total Population)	**95,918**	**92,747**	**188,665**
Under 6	5.9%	6.0%	5.9%
6 to 18	20.7%	19.0%	19.9%
65 and Over	11.6%	10.2%	10.9%
Education (Age 25 and over)	**61,188**	**60,183**	**121,371**
Less than 12 Years	20.7%	17.5%	19.1%
16 Years or More	23.0%	30.9%	26.9%
Urban Population	**100.0%**	**100.0%**	**100.0%**
Family Income (Total Families)	**26,244**	**26,020**	**52,264**
Median Income	$31,156	$30,852	$31,008
Below Poverty Level	.8%	1.1%	.9%
With Children Under 6	.3%	.3%	.3%
With Children 6 to 17	.6%	1.1%	.9%
Headed by Females	.1%	.1%	.1%
Industry (Total Employed)	**50,994**	**53,494**	**104,488**
Professional/Public Admin.	19.5%	23.2%	21.4%
Manufacturing	25.5%	21.2%	23.3%
Retail	16.5%	20.7%	18.6%
Transportation/Communication	8.0%	4.8%	6.4%
Finance/Insurance/Real Estate	8.3%	9.4%	8.8%
Other Service	9.0%	9.0%	9.0%
Housing Units (Total)	**34,107**	**35,414**	**69,521**
Median Value	$84,635	$91,792	$88,213
Owner Occupied	78.4%	69.6%	73.9%
Election Results			
1982 Turnout	47.0%	46.7%	49.6%
Winner	67.2% R	67.0% D	54.8% R
1984 Turnout	61.8%	59.9%	60.9%
Winner	72.9% R	58.8% D	66.1% R
1986 Turnout	41.3%	40.9%	N E
Winner	75.5% R	52.6% D	N E

29

29th
Senate
DISTRICT

House District 57
House District 58

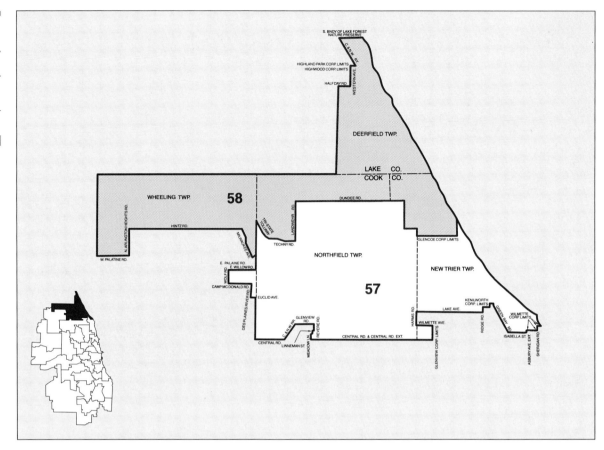

Measured by either median income or median value of owner-occupied housing, Senate District 29 is the most affluent in the state. More than half of its housing is valued over $100,000 and nearly a third at more than $150,000. The district also has a higher percentage of college-educated population than any other district in Illinois.

	H.D. 57	H.D. 58	S.D. 29
Voting Age Population	**64,964**	**67,516**	**132,480**
White	97.4%	94.4%	95.9%
Black	.3%	1.2%	.8%
Hispanic	.9%	3.1%	2.0%
Asian	1.4%	1.3%	1.4%
Age (Total Population)	**96,424**	**97,412**	**193,836**
Under 6	6.6%	7.7%	7.2%
6 to 18	23.8%	23.0%	23.4%
65 and Over	10.3%	7.3%	8.8%
Education (Age 25 and over)	**59,782**	**58,655**	**118,437**
Less than 12 Years	9.0%	13.8%	11.4%
16 Years or More	49.0%	37.6%	43.4%
Urban Population	**100.0%**	**100.0%**	**100.0%**
Family Income (Total Families)	**26,261**	**26,255**	**52,516**
Median Income	$36,579	$34,163	$37,802
Below Poverty Level	.9%	.8%	.9%
With Children Under 6	.3%	.4%	.3%
With Children 6 to 17	.7%	.7%	.7%
Headed by Females	.1%	.0%	.1%
Industry (Total Employed)	**46,054**	**50,173**	**96,227**
Professional/Public Admin.	26.7%	23.6%	25.1%
Manufacturing	18.7%	20.1%	19.4%
Retail	15.6%	18.9%	17.3%
Transportation/Communication	4.8%	5.5%	5.1%
Finance/Insurance/Real Estate	12.6%	9.6%	11.0%
Other Service	11.3%	10.7%	11.0%
Housing Units (Total)	**32,862**	**34,995**	**67,857**
Median Value	$129,984	$107,936	$118,960
Owner Occupied	81.1%	71.3%	76.1%
Election Results			
1982 Turnout	56.1%	45.4%	52.5%
Winner	70.3% R	56.3% D	57.7% R
1984 Turnout	64.5%	60.6%	N E
Winner	76.0% R	51.2% D	N E
1986 Turnout	50.1%	41.0%	46.0%
Winner	77.0% R	66.8% D	60.4% R

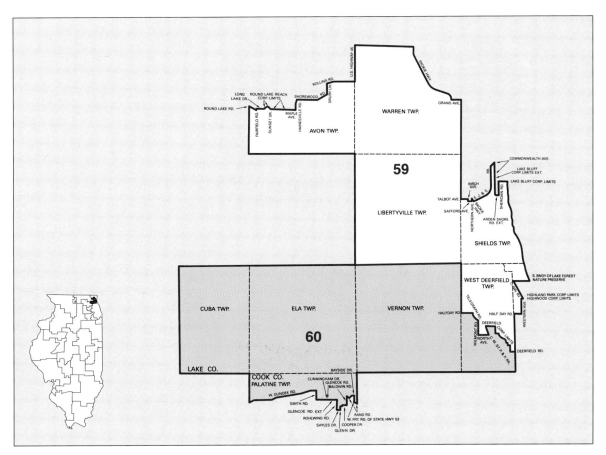

Senate district 30 ranks second in Illinois in median income and third in the median value of its housing units. Just under half of its owner-occupied housing is valued at over $100,000.

	H.D. 59	H.D. 60	S.D. 30
Voting Age Population	**65,236**	**58,344**	**123,580**
White	95.4%	96.0%	95.6%
Black	1.3%	.3%	.8%
Hispanic	2.3%	2.5%	2.4%
Asian	1.0%	1.2%	1.1%
Age (Total Population)	**96,878**	**97,386**	**194,264**
Under 6	8.1%	9.4%	8.8%
6 to 18	23.3%	23.3%	23.3%
65 and Over	7.2%	4.5%	5.8%
Education (Age 25 and over)	**55,531**	**55,929**	**111,460**
Less than 12 Years	17.5%	11.1%	14.3%
16 Years or More	33.7%	38.5%	36.1%
Urban Population	**89.7%**	**86.2%**	**88.0%**
Family Income (Total Families)	**25,325**	**26,071**	**51,396**
Median Income	$31,734	$35,398	$33,514
Below Poverty Level	1.1%	.8%	1.0%
With Children Under 6	.5%	.5%	.5%
With Children 6 to 17	1.0%	1.1%	1.0%
Headed by Females	.2%	.2%	.2%
Industry (Total Employed)	**49,237**	**46,577**	**95,814**
Professional/Public Admin.	24.8%	20.4%	22.6%
Manufacturing	25.8%	23.6%	24.7%
Retail	16.6%	16.6%	16.6%
Transportation/Communication	5.3%	6.2%	5.7%
Finance/Insurance/Real Estate	8.3%	10.4%	9.3%
Other Service	8.5%	9.8%	9.1%
Housing Units (Total)	**33,686**	**34,581**	**68,267**
Median Value	$91,922	$107,831	$99,876
Owner Occupied	74.8%	73.6%	74.2%
Election Results			
1982 Turnout	36.6%	38.4%	46.7%
Winner	100.0% R	100.0% R	53.2% R
1984 Turnout	52.9%	60.6%	N E
Winner	100.0% R	100.0% R	N E
1986 Turnout	33.8%	35.9%	34.7%
Winner	100.0% R	100.0% R	100.0% R

31

31st Senate

DISTRICT

House District 61
House District 62

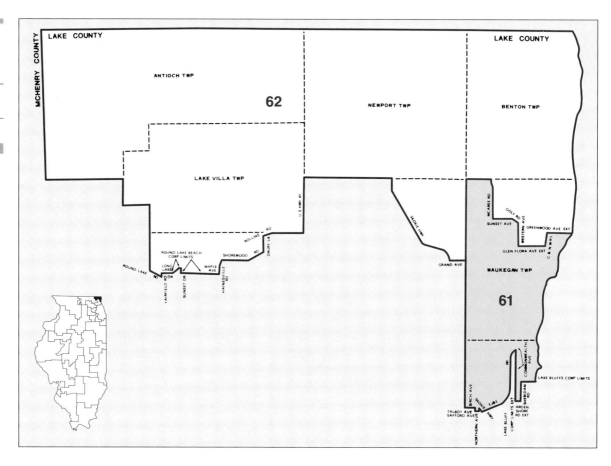

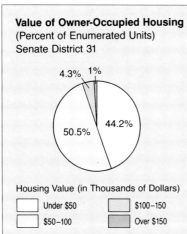

Value of Owner-Occupied Housing
(Percent of Enumerated Units)
Senate District 31

4.3% 1%

44.2%

50.5%

Housing Value (in Thousands of Dollars)

| | Under $50 | | $100–150 |
| | $50–100 | | Over $150 |

	H.D. 61	H.D. 62	S.D. 31
Voting Age Population	**72,122**	**61,070**	**133,192**
White	70.4%	93.5%	81.0%
Black	18.8%	3.4%	11.8%
Hispanic	9.0%	2.6%	6.0%
Asian	1.6%	.6%	1.1%
Age (Total Population)	**96,644**	**97,465**	**194,109**
Under 6	9.4%	10.4%	9.9%
6 to 18	23.0%	24.1%	23.6%
65 and Over	7.6%	7.0%	7.3%
Education (Age 25 and over)	**45,875**	**52,710**	**98,585**
Less than 12 Years	35.6%	28.6%	31.9%
16 Years or More	10.6%	13.0%	11.9%
Urban Population	**99.9%**	**83.8%**	**91.8%**
Family Income (Total Families)	**19,684**	**25,451**	**45,135**
Median Income	$20,195	$25,183	$23,110
Below Poverty Level	3.3%	1.9%	2.5%
With Children Under 6	2.3%	1.0%	1.6%
With Children 6 to 17	2.3%	1.8%	2.0%
Headed by Females	1.1%	.6%	.8%
Industry (Total Employed)	**33,233**	**44,893**	**78,126**
Professional/Public Admin.	27.6%	20.3%	23.4%
Manufacturing	32.9%	33.7%	33.4%
Retail	15.0%	15.8%	15.5%
Transportation/Communication	6.2%	6.4%	6.3%
Finance/Insurance/Real Estate	3.9%	4.9%	4.5%
Other Service	7.1%	6.5%	6.8%
Housing Units (Total)	**29,448**	**35,092**	**64,540**
Median Value	$47,609	$57,694	$52,651
Owner Occupied	46.3%	70.6%	59.5%
Election Results			
1982 Turnout	17.2%	37.3%	29.4%
Winner	100.0% D	62.1% R	65.7% R
1984 Turnout	28.6%	55.4%	41.3%
Winner	68.2% D	64.9% R	68.7% R
1986 Turnout	16.4%	26.3%	N E
Winner	73.2% D	100.0% R	N E

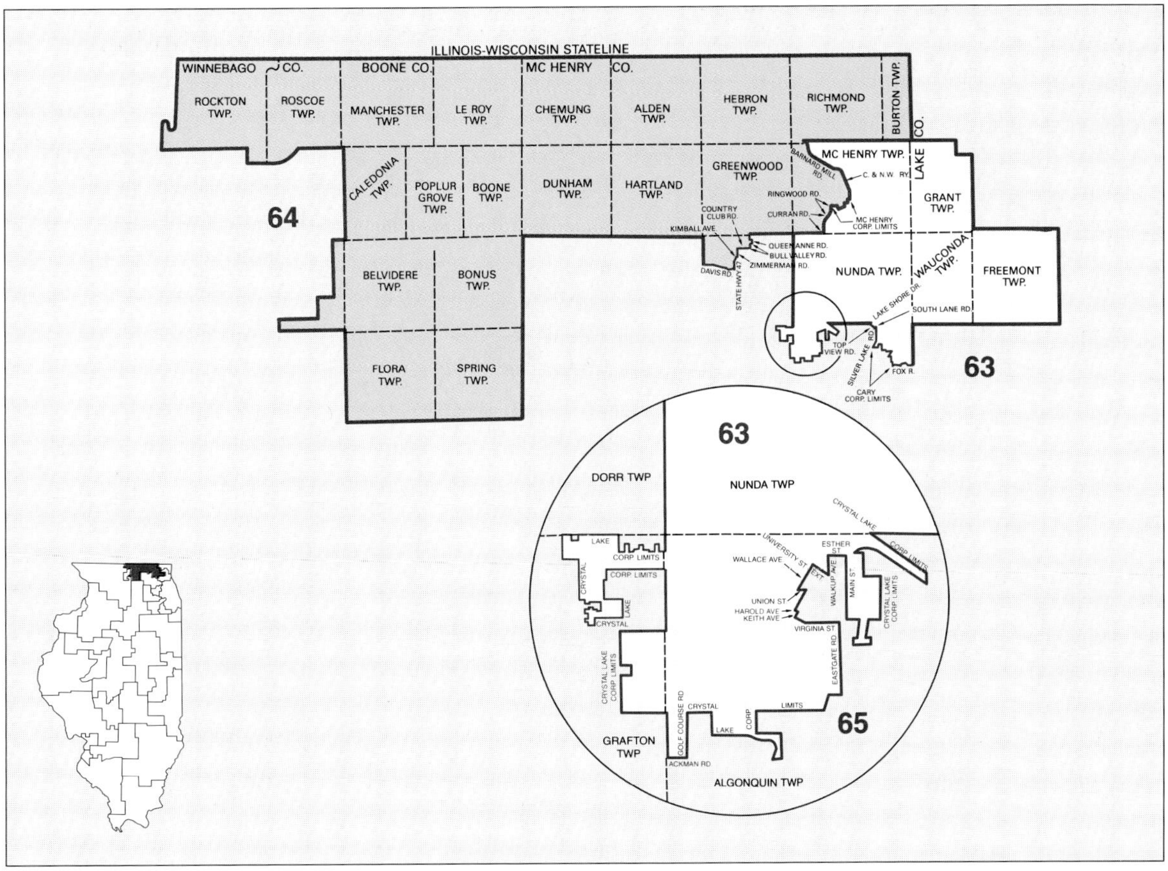
ILLINOIS-WISCONSIN STATELINE
WINNEBAGO CO.
BOONE CO.
MC HENRY CO.
ROCKTON TWP.
ROSCOE TWP.
MANCHESTER TWP.
LE ROY TWP.
CHEMUNG TWP.
ALDEN TWP.
HEBRON TWP.
RICHMOND TWP.
BURTON TWP.
LAKE CO.
MC HENRY TWP.
CALEDONIA TWP.
POPLUR GROVE TWP.
BOONE TWP.
DUNHAM TWP.
HARTLAND TWP.
GREENWOOD TWP.
GRANT TWP.
64
BELVIDERE TWP.
BONUS TWP.
NUNDA TWP.
WAUCONDA TWP.
FREEMONT TWP.
FLORA TWP.
SPRING TWP.
63
DORR TWP
NUNDA TWP
GRAFTON TWP
ALGONQUIN TWP
65

32nd Senate DISTRICT

House District 63
House District 64

Place of Residence
(Percent of Total Population)
Senate District 32

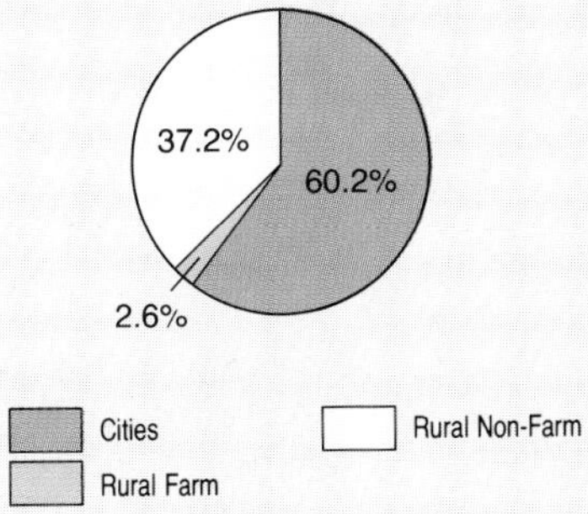
37.2%
60.2%
2.6%
Cities
Rural Farm
Rural Non-Farm

	H.D. 63	H.D. 64	S.D. 32
Voting Age Population	**66,571**	**62,003**	**128,574**
White	98.5%	96.8%	97.7%
Black	.0%	.7%	.4%
Hispanic	1.3%	2.2%	1.7%
Asian	.2%	.2%	.2%
Age (Total Population)	**94,197**	**91,544**	**185,741**
Under 6	9.1%	8.9%	9.0%
6 to 18	23.4%	23.4%	23.4%
65 and Over	8.7%	9.7%	9.2%
Education (Age 25 and over)	**52,723**	**52,676**	**105,399**
Less than 12 Years	27.9%	29.6%	28.8%
16 Years or More	19.1%	12.9%	16.0%
Urban Population	**66.7%**	**55.8%**	**61.3%**
Family Income (Total Families)	**24,727**	**24,728**	**49,455**
Median Income	$25,995	$23,428	$24,821
Below Poverty Level	1.8%	1.9%	1.9%
With Children Under 6	.8%	.9%	.9%
With Children 6 to 17	1.1%	1.5%	1.3%
Headed by Females	.3%	.3%	.3%
Industry (Total Employed)	**49,342**	**42,682**	**92,024**
Professional/Public Admin.	17.9%	17.0%	17.5%
Manufacturing	29.6%	38.6%	33.8%
Retail	17.0%	14.9%	16.0%
Transportation/Communication	7.6%	5.5%	6.6%
Finance/Insurance/Real Estate	6.5%	5.2%	5.9%
Other Service	7.7%	5.5%	6.7%
Housing Units (Total)	**34,178**	**32,913**	**67,091**
Median Value	$66,455	$55,887	$61,171
Owner Occupied	73.9%	68.4%	71.2%
Election Results			
1982 Turnout	38.9%	44.0%	41.5%
Winner	72.1% R	64.7% R	71.2% R
1984 Turnout	48.3%	48.2%	N E
Winner	100.0% R	100.0% R	N E
1986 Turnout	35.1%	36.1%	35.9%
Winner	100.0% R	100.0% R	100.0% R

33rd
Senate
DISTRICT

House District 65
House District 66

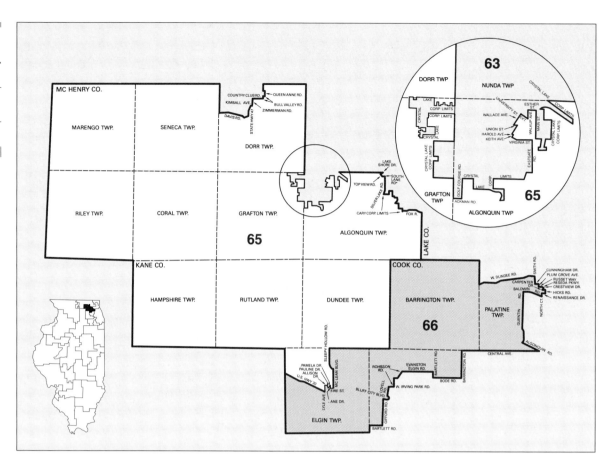

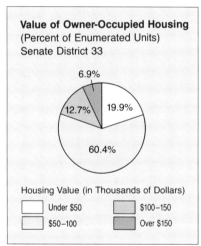

Value of Owner-Occupied Housing
(Percent of Enumerated Units)
Senate District 33

6.9%
12.7%
19.9%
60.4%

Housing Value (in Thousands of Dollars)

- Under $50
- $50–100
- $100–150
- Over $150

Senate District 33 ranks in the top third of the state's senate districts in median value of owner-occupied housing, and it ranks in the bottom third in the proportion of its population age sixty-five and over.

	H.D. 65	H.D. 66	S.D. 33
Voting Age Population	54,251	64,555	118,806
White	96.0%	89.4%	92.4%
Black	.2%	3.4%	2.0%
Hispanic	3.4%	6.1%	4.9%
Asian	.3%	1.1%	.8%
Age (Total Population)	96,847	96,902	193,749
Under 6	9.8%	10.0%	9.9%
6 to 18	24.8%	21.1%	23.0%
65 and Over	6.3%	9.3%	7.8%
Education (Age 25 and over)	52,744	55,140	107,884
Less than 12 Years	23.2%	25.3%	24.3%
16 Years or More	15.6%	22.0%	18.9%
Urban Population	71.1%	96.0%	83.5%
Family Income (Total Families)	25,396	24,851	50,247
Median Income	$26,352	$26,173	$26,267
Below Poverty Level	1.5%	1.9%	1.7%
With Children Under 6	.7%	1.0%	.9%
With Children 6 to 17	1.3%	1.3%	1.3%
Headed by Females	.5%	.6%	.5%
Industry (Total Employed)	43,077	45,144	88,221
Professional/Public Admin.	16.4%	22.7%	19.6%
Manufacturing	33.4%	29.9%	31.6%
Retail	15.0%	15.5%	15.3%
Transportation/Communication	8.4%	6.5%	7.4%
Finance/Insurance/Real Estate	5.9%	7.0%	6.5%
Other Service	6.9%	7.6%	7.2%
Housing Units (Total)	32,534	35,870	68,404
Median Value	$68,157	$72,653	$70,405
Owner Occupied	73.9%	61.9%	67.6%
Election Results			
1982 Turnout	38.0%	36.7%	40.6%
Winner	99.9% R	72.1% R	70.2% R
1984 Turnout	57.7%	53.7%	N E
Winner	100.0% R	71.3% R	N E
1986 Turnout	38.3%	30.4%	38.7%
Winner	100.0% R	100.0% R	76.0% R

34

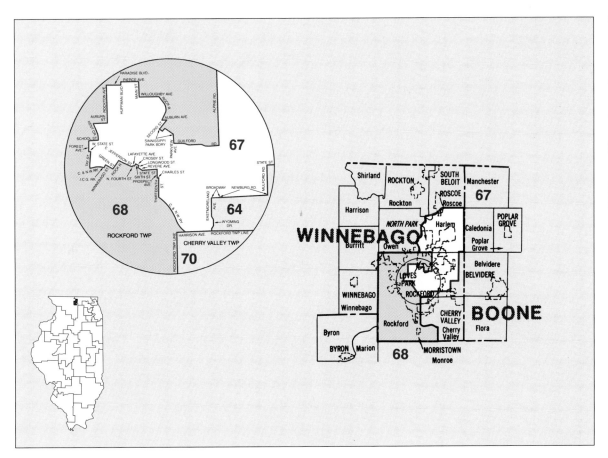

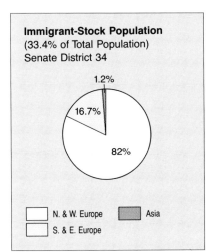

Immigrant-Stock Population
(33.4% of Total Population)
Senate District 34

1.2%
16.7%
82%

N. & W. Europe   Asia
S. & E. Europe

	H.D. 67	H.D. 68	S.D. 34
Voting Age Population	**67,148**	**60,920**	**128,068**
White	95.1%	83.8%	89.7%
Black	3.5%	13.8%	8.4%
Hispanic	1.0%	2.4%	1.7%
Asian	.3%	.0%	.2%
Age (Total Population)	**97,657**	**95,352**	**193,009**
Under 6	8.8%	8.9%	8.8%
6 to 18	21.9%	21.8%	21.9%
65 and Over	11.0%	10.9%	11.0%
Education (Age 25 and over)	**57,387**	**53,974**	**111,361**
Less than 12 Years	29.0%	41.2%	34.9%
16 Years or More	17.4%	8.9%	13.3%
Urban Population	**96.5%**	**93.7%**	**95.1%**
Family Income (Total Families)	**25,950**	**25,117**	**51,067**
Median Income	$24,044	$20,611	$22,356
Below Poverty Level	2.7%	4.0%	3.3%
With Children Under 6	1.4%	2.1%	1.8%
With Children 6 to 17	1.8%	3.0%	2.3%
Headed by Females	.8%	1.6%	1.2%
Industry (Total Employed)	**47,348**	**40,993**	**88,341**
Professional/Public Admin.	21.1%	17.0%	19.2%
Manufacturing	36.4%	45.1%	40.4%
Retail	17.9%	14.2%	16.2%
Transportation/Communication	4.6%	5.3%	4.9%
Finance/Insurance/Real Estate	5.3%	3.7%	4.6%
Other Service	6.3%	7.3%	6.8%
Housing Units (Total)	**36,315**	**36,483**	**72,798**
Median Value	$45,162	$35,359	$40,260
Owner Occupied	68.9%	60.9%	64.8%
Election Results			
1982 Turnout	36.7%	43.6%	45.8%
Winner	100.0% R	64.0% D	55.5% D
1984 Turnout	49.4%	60.5%	63.6%
Winner	100.0% R	67.1% D	51.5% D
1986 Turnout	33.5%	33.8%	N E
Winner	100.0% R	66.4% D	N E

35

35th Senate

DISTRICT

House District 69
House District 70

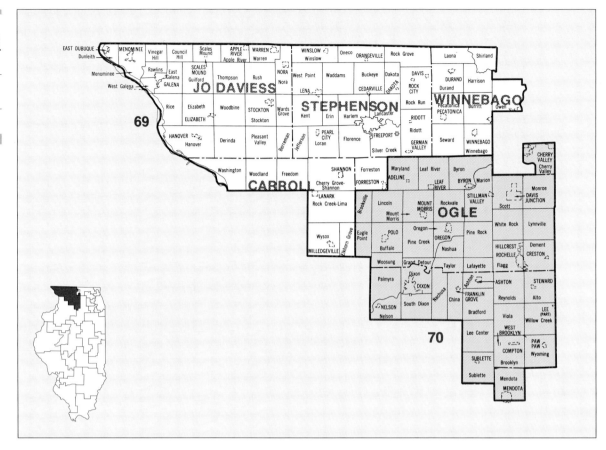

Senate District 35 is a mixed urban and rural district. Most of House District 70's population lives in cities, while two-thirds of the people in House District 69 are rural, mostly non-farm.

	H.D. 69	H.D. 70	S.D. 35
Voting Age Population	**61,529**	**63,820**	**125,349**
White	96.9%	97.1%	97.1%
Black	2.6%	1.0%	1.8%
Hispanic	.3%	1.6%	1.0%
Asian	.1%	.2%	.2%
Age (Total Population)	**97,228**	**96,484**	**193,712**
Under 6	8.5%	8.9%	8.7%
6 to 18	22.6%	22.6%	22.6%
65 and Over	13.1%	11.1%	12.1%
Education (Age 25 and over)	**57,742**	**56,187**	**113,929**
Less than 12 Years	32.4%	30.6%	31.5%
16 Years or More	10.7%	11.6%	11.1%
Urban Population	**34.0%**	**51.6%**	**42.8%**
Family Income (Total Families)	**26,600**	**25,747**	**52,347**
Median Income	$20,837	$22,231	$21,561
Below Poverty Level	3.0%	2.3%	2.6%
With Children Under 6	1.0%	.9%	.9%
With Children 6 to 17	1.8%	1.7%	1.7%
Headed by Females	.3%	.3%	.3%
Industry (Total Employed)	**45,436**	**44,587**	**90,023**
Professional/Public Admin.	18.0%	20.6%	19.3%
Manufacturing	32.1%	33.8%	32.9%
Retail	13.0%	14.2%	13.6%
Transportation/Communication	5.1%	6.9%	6.0%
Finance/Insurance/Real Estate	6.4%	4.2%	5.3%
Other Service	5.5%	4.9%	5.2%
Housing Units (Total)	**37,564**	**35,743**	**73,307**
Median Value	$39,902	$44,264	$42,083
Owner Occupied	68.8%	65.6%	67.3%
Election Results			
1982 Turnout	50.7%	35.4%	48.3%
Winner	53.4% D	100.0% R	53.4% R
1984 Turnout	64.3%	58.6%	N E
Winner	63.4% D	68.9% R	N E
1986 Turnout	50.0%	32.9%	36.2%
Winner	60.0% D	100.0% R	100.0% R

36

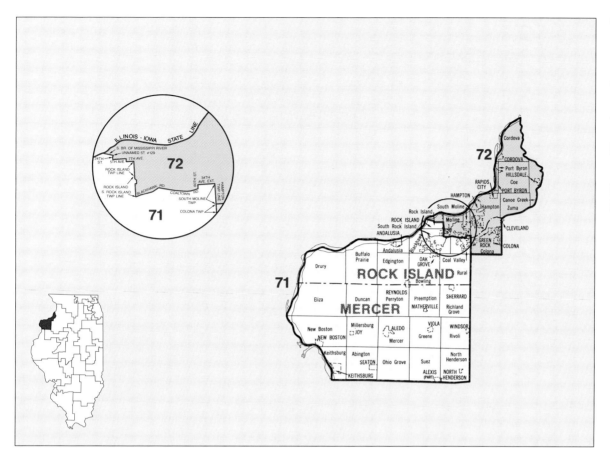

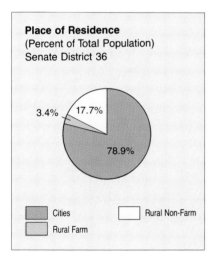

Place of Residence
(Percent of Total Population)
Senate District 36

3.4%   17.7%

78.9%

Cities	Rural Non-Farm
Rural Farm	

Senate District 36, bordering the Mississippi River, includes the Quad Cities.

	H.D. 71	H.D. 72	S.D. 36
Voting Age Population	**64,757**	**67,463**	**132,220**
White	91.9%	92.9%	92.4%
Black	6.3%	2.1%	4.1%
Hispanic	1.6%	4.6%	3.1%
Asian	.2%	.3%	.3%
Age (Total Population)	**96,577**	**96,293**	**192,870**
Under 6	9.4%	9.1%	9.3%
6 to 18	21.6%	20.9%	21.3%
65 and Over	11.7%	11.1%	11.4%
Education (Age 25 and over)	**55,975**	**55,748**	**111,723**
Less than 12 Years	31.2%	30.4%	30.8%
16 Years or More	11.3%	12.1%	11.7%
Urban Population	**70.3%**	**87.5%**	**78.9%**
Family Income (Total Families)	**25,833**	**25,770**	**51,603**
Median Income	$22,508	$23,269	$22,871
Below Poverty Level	3.4%	2.7%	3.1%
With Children Under 6	1.7%	1.5%	1.6%
With Children 6 to 17	2.1%	1.5%	1.8%
Headed by Females	1.2%	.7%	1.0%
Industry (Total Employed)	**43,467**	**42,456**	**85,923**
Professional/Public Admin.	24.5%	21.6%	23.1%
Manufacturing	27.5%	34.3%	30.8%
Retail	15.8%	16.1%	16.0%
Transportation/Communication	6.8%	6.2%	6.5%
Finance/Insurance/Real Estate	4.7%	4.6%	4.6%
Other Service	6.3%	6.3%	6.3%
Housing Units (Total)	**36,901**	**36,751**	**73,652**
Median Value	$45,291	$47,373	$46,332
Owner Occupied	67.4%	67.0%	67.2%
Election Results			
1982 Turnout	50.3%	49.0%	49.8%
Winner	60.7% D	54.5% D	62.2% D
1984 Turnout	46.9%	64.3%	N E
Winner	100.0% D	57.8% D	N E
1986 Turnout	40.7%	40.4%	40.6%
Winner	74.3% D	63.4% D	64.3% D

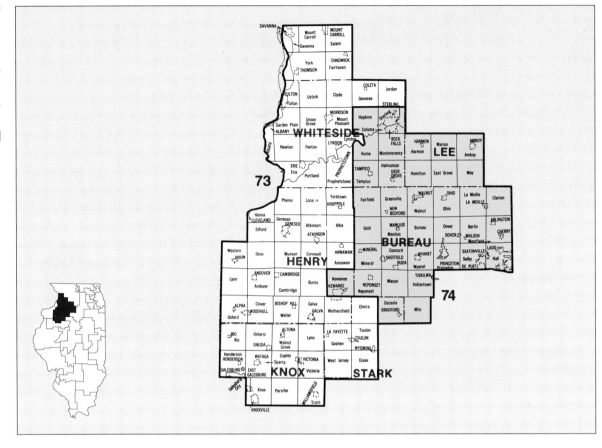

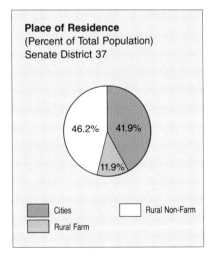

Place of Residence
(Percent of Total Population)
Senate District 37

46.2%   41.9%

11.9%

Cities   Rural Non-Farm
Rural Farm

With two-thirds of its housing units valued under $50,000, Senate District 37 ranks in the bottom third among the state's senate districts in median value of owner-occupied housing.

	H.D. 73	H.D. 74	S.D. 37
Voting Age Population	**57,982**	**64,246**	**122,228**
White	99.0%	94.4%	96.6%
Black	.3%	.7%	.5%
Hispanic	.6%	4.6%	2.7%
Asian	.1%	.2%	.1%
Age (Total Population)	**95,995**	**96,284**	**192,279**
Under 6	9.0%	9.1%	9.0%
6 to 18	22.1%	22.3%	22.2%
65 and Over	13.7%	13.8%	13.7%
Education (Age 25 and over)	**57,540**	**56,662**	**114,202**
Less than 12 Years	31.8%	36.6%	34.2%
16 Years or More	10.5%	9.8%	10.1%
Urban Population	**31.3%**	**52.6%**	**41.9%**
Family Income (Total Families)	**26,614**	**26,117**	**52,731**
Median Income	$21,433	$21,332	$21,387
Below Poverty Level	2.9%	2.9%	2.9%
With Children Under 6	1.1%	1.2%	1.2%
With Children 6 to 17	1.9%	1.8%	1.9%
Headed by Females	.4%	.7%	.5%
Industry (Total Employed)	**41,162**	**40,924**	**82,086**
Professional/Public Admin.	19.3%	19.6%	19.4%
Manufacturing	28.6%	34.0%	31.3%
Retail	13.9%	15.5%	14.7%
Transportation/Communication	7.4%	6.2%	6.8%
Finance/Insurance/Real Estate	4.0%	4.1%	4.0%
Other Service	4.9%	5.5%	5.2%
Housing Units (Total)	**36,303**	**36,686**	**72,989**
Median Value	$42,237	$36,493	$39,365
Owner Occupied	71.0%	68.6%	69.8%
Election Results			
1982 Turnout	53.6%	51.4%	52.5%
Winner	65.4% R	63.4% D	53.4% R
1984 Turnout	69.2%	65.2%	67.3%
Winner	63.4% R	63.0% D	58.6% R
1986 Turnout	50.0%	43.8%	N E
Winner	68.7% R	67.9% D	N E

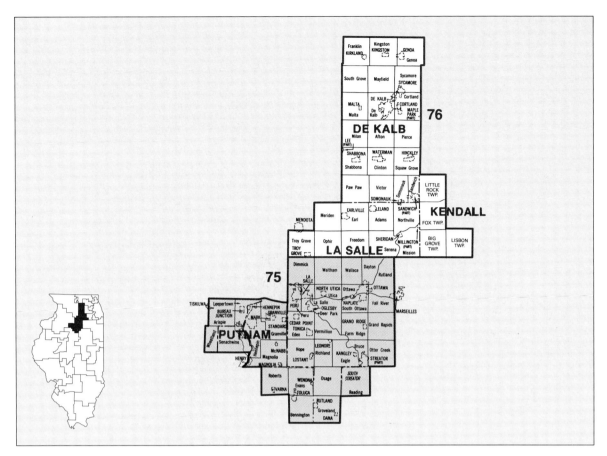

Over 14 percent of the work force in House District 76 is employed by the state government, mainly reflecting the presence of Northern Illinois University in the City of DeKalb.

	H.D. 75	H.D. 76	S.D. 38
Voting Age Population	70,570	71,988	142,558
White	97.9%	95.1%	96.5%
Black	.3%	2.2%	1.2%
Hispanic	1.6%	1.9%	1.7%
Asian	.2%	.8%	.5%
Age (Total Population)	99,476	97,309	196,785
Under 6	8.2%	7.9%	8.0%
6 to 18	20.9%	20.5%	20.7%
65 and Over	14.9%	8.9%	11.9%
Education (Age 25 and over)	60,654	48,904	109,558
Less than 12 Years	38.6%	26.6%	33.2%
16 Years or More	8.8%	18.9%	13.3%
Urban Population	60.3%	57.8%	59.1%
Family Income (Total Families)	27,194	22,345	49,539
Median Income	$21,680	$22,758	$22,153
Below Poverty Level	2.9%	2.4%	2.7%
With Children Under 6	1.1%	1.2%	1.2%
With Children 6 to 17	1.6%	1.4%	1.5%
Headed by Females	.7%	.4%	.6%
Industry (Total Employed)	42,214	45,245	87,459
Professional/Public Admin.	20.2%	29.5%	25.0%
Manufacturing	29.0%	26.9%	27.9%
Retail	18.6%	15.3%	16.9%
Transportation/Communication	7.9%	5.3%	6.5%
Finance/Insurance/Real Estate	3.7%	4.0%	3.9%
Other Service	5.9%	5.0%	5.4%
Housing Units (Total)	39,074	33,327	72,401
Median Value	$40,963	$54,356	$47,659
Owner Occupied	69.1%	58.0%	64.0%
Election Results			
1982 Turnout	51.3%	38.1%	44.9%
Winner	58.1% D	62.5% R	52.4% D
1984 Turnout	61.4%	55.3%	N E
Winner	65.0% D	58.5% R	N E
1986 Turnout	36.7%	36.2%	40.7%
Winner	100.0% D	62.0% R	51.6% D

39th
Senate
DISTRICT

House District 77
House District 78

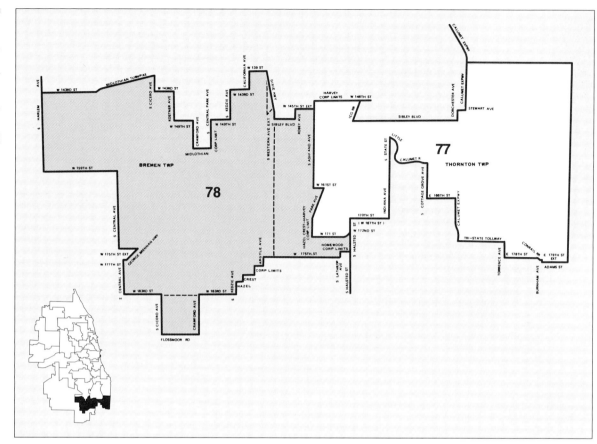

While 53.9 percent of the immigrant-stock population in House District 77 traces its roots to Southern and Eastern Europe, 62.4 percent of the corresponding category in House District 78 is of Northern and Western European origins.

	H.D. 77	H.D. 78	S.D. 39
Voting Age Population	**68,625**	**55,864**	**124,489**
White	82.5%	69.7%	76.8%
Black	13.8%	27.8%	20.1%
Hispanic	3.4%	1.6%	2.6%
Asian	.3%	.9%	.6%
Age (Total Population)	**96,659**	**96,943**	**193,602**
Under 6	8.0%	10.6%	9.3%
6 to 18	20.6%	26.4%	23.5%
65 and Over	10.3%	5.7%	8.0%
Education (Age 25 and over)	**57,422**	**50,918**	**108,340**
Less than 12 Years	34.8%	27.7%	31.5%
16 Years or More	9.8%	11.0%	10.4%
Urban Population	**100.0%**	**99.5%**	**99.7%**
Family Income (Total Families)	**25,735**	**23,922**	**49,657**
Median Income	$25,464	$25,690	$25,574
Below Poverty Level	2.5%	2.4%	2.5%
With Children Under 6	1.1%	1.5%	1.3%
With Children 6 to 17	2.5%	2.4%	2.5%
Headed by Females	.9%	.9%	.9%
Industry (Total Employed)	**44,822**	**38,634**	**83,456**
Professional/Public Admin.	19.9%	22.6%	21.2%
Manufacturing	30.3%	24.7%	27.7%
Retail	17.7%	18.2%	17.9%
Transportation/Communication	9.6%	11.4%	10.4%
Finance/Insurance/Real Estate	6.5%	6.8%	6.6%
Other Service	6.8%	6.7%	6.7%
Housing Units (Total)	**35,418**	**29,505**	**64,923**
Median Value	$49,391	$52,983	$51,187
Owner Occupied	65.5%	77.4%	70.9%
Election Results			
1982 Turnout	40.5%	44.3%	44.0%
Winner	61.8% D	64.9% D	66.3% D
1984 Turnout	47.3%	54.5%	N E
Winner	65.1% D	63.1% D	N E
1986 Turnout	31.8%	27.2%	32.3%
Winner	59.9% D	100.0% D	69.8% D

40

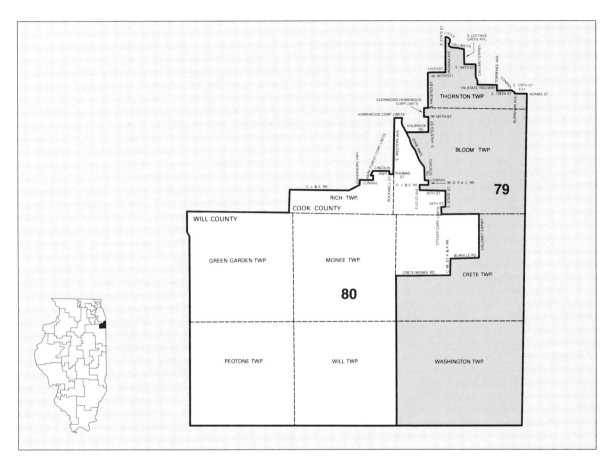

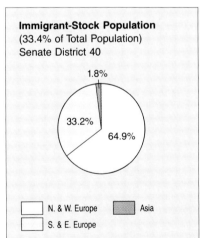

Immigrant-Stock Population
(33.4% of Total Population)
Senate District 40

1.8%
33.2%
64.9%

	N. & W. Europe	Asia
	S. & E. Europe	

	H.D. 79	H.D. 80	S.D. 40
Voting Age Population	**69,754**	**60,974**	**130,728**
White	85.7%	84.7%	85.3%
Black	10.5%	11.3%	10.9%
Hispanic	3.6%	3.4%	3.5%
Asian	.2%	.5%	.4%
Age (Total Population)	**100,592**	**93,130**	**193,722**
Under 6	9.0%	9.6%	9.3%
6 to 18	24.4%	23.2%	23.8%
65 and Over	8.5%	7.5%	8.0%
Education (Age 25 and over)	**56,073**	**52,204**	**108,277**
Less than 12 Years	33.6%	23.4%	28.7%
16 Years or More	13.0%	18.8%	15.8%
Urban Population	**89.8%**	**93.1%**	**91.4%**
Family Income (Total Families)	**26,206**	**24,779**	**50,985**
Median Income	$26,307	$24,343	$25,393
Below Poverty Level	2.9%	2.1%	2.5%
With Children Under 6	1.4%	1.3%	1.3%
With Children 6 to 17	2.3%	1.7%	2.0%
Headed by Females	1.0%	.9%	1.0%
Industry (Total Employed)	**45,495**	**41,770**	**87,265**
Professional/Public Admin.	20.4%	24.2%	22.2%
Manufacturing	27.7%	26.0%	26.9%
Retail	17.6%	17.1%	17.4%
Transportation/Communication	9.1%	8.8%	8.9%
Finance/Insurance/Real Estate	6.3%	6.7%	6.5%
Other Service	7.2%	7.2%	7.2%
Housing Units (Total)	**33,156**	**32,929**	**66,085**
Median Value	$58,090	$52,069	$55,079
Owner Occupied	73.8%	64.4%	69.1%
Election Results			
1982 Turnout	41.2%	43.1%	43.3%
Winner	57.9% R	51.1% D	64.6% R
1984 Turnout	54.2%	56.6%	55.5%
Winner	63.9% R	51.5% R	64.8% R
1986 Turnout	34.2%	37.0%	N E
Winner	67.5% R	56.4% R	N E

41

41st
Senate
DISTRICT

House District 81
House District 82

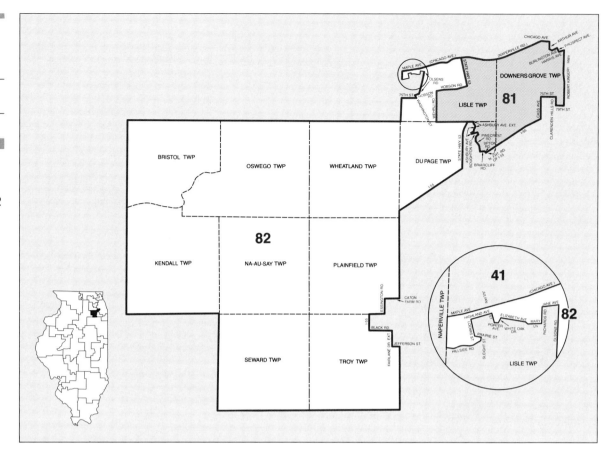

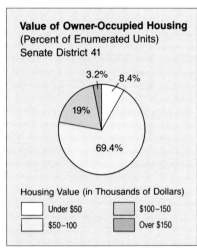

Value of Owner-Occupied Housing
(Percent of Enumerated Units)
Senate District 41

3.2%   8.4%

19%

69.4%

Housing Value (in Thousands of Dollars)

☐ Under $50	☐ $100–150	
☐ $50–100	■ Over $150	

Senate District 41 ranks eighth in the state in median value of owner-occupied housing, seventh in median income, and sixth in the proportion of population with college degrees. It also has the second-lowest proportion of population age sixty-five and over.

	H.D. 81	H.D. 82	S.D. 41
Voting Age Population	**67,665**	**60,904**	**128,569**
White	93.9%	95.5%	94.7%
Black	1.7%	1.6%	1.6%
Hispanic	1.5%	1.6%	1.5%
Asian	2.9%	1.3%	2.1%
Age (Total Population)	**97,299**	**97,097**	**194,396**
Under 6	9.1%	11.2%	10.1%
6 to 18	22.2%	25.8%	24.0%
65 and Over	5.6%	4.1%	4.9%
Education (Age 25 and over)	**56,419**	**51,942**	**108,361**
Less than 12 Years	14.8%	15.3%	15.0%
16 Years or More	30.8%	26.0%	28.5%
Urban Population	**98.7%**	**79.8%**	**89.2%**
Family Income (Total Families)	**25,974**	**24,889**	**50,863**
Median Income	$30,569	$29,758	$30,159
Below Poverty Level	1.0%	1.1%	1.0%
With Children Under 6	.3%	.5%	.4%
With Children 6 to 17	.8%	.9%	.8%
Headed by Females	.1%	.3%	.2%
Industry (Total Employed)	**53,050**	**46,483**	**99,533**
Professional/Public Admin.	21.1%	20.0%	20.6%
Manufacturing	23.8%	27.9%	25.7%
Retail	17.1%	16.3%	16.7%
Transportation/Communication	8.4%	8.7%	8.5%
Finance/Insurance/Real Estate	9.0%	7.3%	8.2%
Other Service	9.9%	7.6%	8.8%
Housing Units (Total)	**35,845**	**32,470**	**68,315**
Median Value	$81,051	$74,354	$77,702
Owner Occupied	66.9%	73.2%	69.9%
Election Results			
1982 Turnout	41.6%	44.9%	42.9%
Winner	65.2% R	67.8% R	65.1% R
1984 Turnout	46.0%	54.4%	N E
Winner	100.0% R	100.0% R	N E
1986 Turnout	38.8%	36.4%	40.2%
Winner	74.8% R	100.0% R	72.9% R

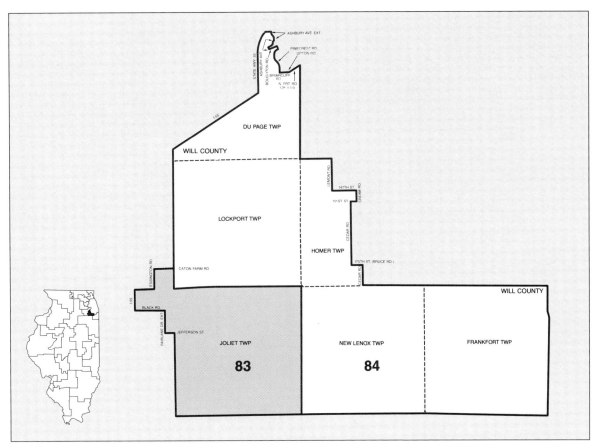

42nd

Senate

DISTRICT

House District 83
House District 84

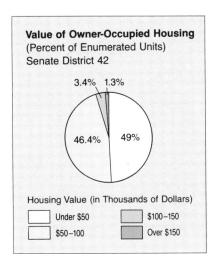

Value of Owner-Occupied Housing
(Percent of Enumerated Units)
Senate District 42

3.4%   1.3%

46.4%   49%

Housing Value (in Thousands of Dollars)

☐ Under $50	☐ $100–150
☐ $50–100	☐ Over $150

	H.D. 83	H.D. 84	S.D. 42
Voting Age Population	**64,119**	**56,610**	**120,729**
White	77.2%	88.9%	82.7%
Black	16.6%	7.5%	12.3%
Hispanic	6.1%	3.0%	4.7%
Asian	.1%	.5%	.3%
Age (Total Population)	**96,393**	**97,625**	**194,018**
Under 6	9.8%	10.5%	10.2%
6 to 18	20.9%	25.5%	23.2%
65 and Over	12.3%	4.8%	8.5%
Education (Age 25 and over)	**54,100**	**50,807**	**104,907**
Less than 12 Years	40.0%	28.1%	34.2%
16 Years or More	11.4%	12.3%	11.8%
Urban Population	**99.0%**	**76.4%**	**87.7%**
Family Income (Total Families)	**23,716**	**24,185**	**47,901**
Median Income	$22,530	$26,330	$24,718
Below Poverty Level	3.5%	1.5%	2.5%
With Children Under 6	1.7%	.7%	1.2%
With Children 6 to 17	3.1%	1.0%	2.0%
Headed by Females	1.4%	.4%	.9%
Industry (Total Employed)	**39,201**	**40,902**	**80,103**
Professional/Public Admin.	24.7%	19.7%	22.1%
Manufacturing	30.1%	29.7%	29.9%
Retail	15.6%	17.2%	16.4%
Transportation/Communication	9.4%	9.0%	9.2%
Finance/Insurance/Real Estate	4.6%	4.7%	4.7%
Other Service	6.6%	7.5%	7.1%
Housing Units (Total)	**36,481**	**29,689**	**66,170**
Median Value	$43,312	$58,719	$51,015
Owner Occupied	58.5%	79.4%	67.9%
Election Results			
1982 Turnout	45.6%	46.0%	46.1%
Winner	60.0% D	54.9% R	70.2% D
1984 Turnout	55.0%	62.3%	N E
Winner	61.8% D	59.5% R	N E
1986 Turnout	35.4%	40.3%	38.6%
Winner	55.6% D	52.4% R	54.6% D

43

43rd

Senate

DISTRICT

House District 85
House District 86

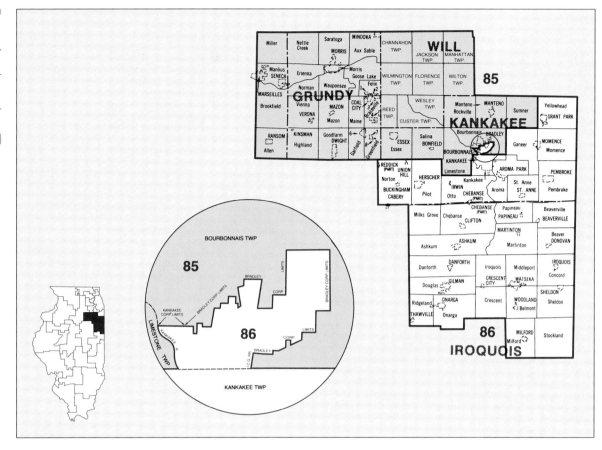

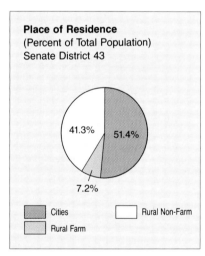

Place of Residence
(Percent of Total Population)
Senate District 43

- 51.4% Cities
- 41.3% Rural Non-Farm
- 7.2% Rural Farm

Cities | Rural Non-Farm
Rural Farm

Senate District 43 is a mixed urban and rural district, in which three-fifths of the owner-occupied housing is valued under $50,000. The district also ranks in the bottom third among Illinois senate districts in the proportion of college graduates in its population.

	H.D. 85	H.D. 86	S.D. 43
Voting Age Population	**63,647**	**61,185**	**124,832**
White	98.0%	85.4%	91.8%
Black	1.0%	13.2%	7.0%
Hispanic	.8%	1.2%	1.0%
Asian	.2%	.1%	.2%
Age (Total Population)	**92,248**	**99,954**	**192,202**
Under 6	9.9%	9.5%	9.7%
6 to 18	23.6%	22.4%	23.0%
65 and Over	8.8%	13.2%	11.1%
Education (Age 25 and over)	**51,423**	**57,920**	**109,343**
Less than 12 Years	35.7%	38.6%	37.2%
16 Years or More	10.4%	9.1%	9.7%
Urban Population	**48.3%**	**54.3%**	**51.4%**
Family Income (Total Families)	**24,325**	**26,161**	**50,486**
Median Income	$23,916	$18,780	$21,365
Below Poverty Level	2.6%	4.9%	3.8%
With Children Under 6	.9%	2.0%	1.5%
With Children 6 to 17	1.7%	3.5%	2.6%
Headed by Females	.6%	1.7%	1.1%
Industry (Total Employed)	**41,533**	**37,777**	**79,310**
Professional/Public Admin.	20.5%	23.7%	22.0%
Manufacturing	30.5%	28.2%	29.4%
Retail	15.8%	14.9%	15.4%
Transportation/Communication	8.7%	6.1%	7.4%
Finance/Insurance/Real Estate	4.0%	4.1%	4.1%
Other Service	5.7%	6.5%	6.1%
Housing Units (Total)	**32,639**	**38,933**	**71,572**
Median Value	$50,619	$36,302	$43,460
Owner Occupied	68.5%	61.9%	64.9%
Election Results			
1982 Turnout	49.2%	54.1%	51.5%
Winner	57.2% D	53.7% D	59.8% D
1984 Turnout	60.1%	64.3%	61.6%
Winner	53.6% D	56.9% D	58.0% D
1986 Turnout	44.7%	43.3%	N E
Winner	50.1% R	66.0% D	N E

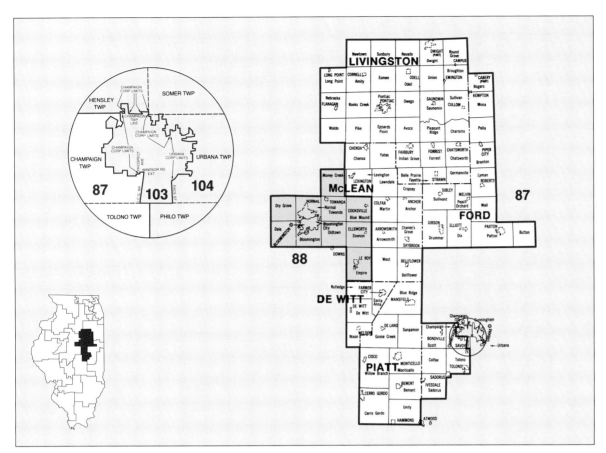

The presence of Illinois State University in House District 88 largely accounts for the high proportion (11.2%) of state government employees among its work force.

	H.D. 87	H.D. 88	S.D. 44
Voting Age Population	**65,786**	**74,159**	**139,945**
White	95.1%	93.5%	94.3%
Black	3.9%	4.8%	4.4%
Hispanic	.7%	.8%	.8%
Asian	.3%	.8%	.5%
Age (Total Population)	**98,030**	**96,312**	**194,342**
Under 6	8.6%	7.9%	8.3%
6 to 18	20.9%	19.3%	20.1%
65 and Over	13.2%	9.0%	11.1%
Education (Age 25 and over)	**58,703**	**48,329**	**107,032**
Less than 12 Years	32.6%	22.2%	27.9%
16 Years or More	15.6%	25.8%	20.2%
Urban Population	**38.8%**	**88.5%**	**63.4%**
Family Income (Total Families)	**26,468**	**21,684**	**48,152**
Median Income	$21,930	$23,581	$22,545
Below Poverty Level	2.9%	2.0%	2.5%
With Children Under 6	1.1%	1.5%	1.3%
With Children 6 to 17	1.5%	1.8%	1.6%
Headed by Females	.5%	.5%	.5%
Industry (Total Employed)	**47,077**	**47,138**	**94,215**
Professional/Public Admin.	26.0%	29.0%	27.5%
Manufacturing	19.4%	12.1%	15.8%
Retail	15.7%	20.1%	17.9%
Transportation/Communication	6.8%	6.3%	6.5%
Finance/Insurance/Real Estate	5.5%	14.9%	10.2%
Other Service	5.5%	6.6%	6.1%
Housing Units (Total)	**37,478**	**36,677**	**74,155**
Median Value	$41,199	$53,557	$47,378
Owner Occupied	66.3%	56.8%	61.6%
Election Results			
1982 Turnout	39.0%	28.4%	41.7%
Winner	100.0% R	99.9% R	67.7% R
1984 Turnout	47.7%	39.0%	N E
Winner	100.0% R	99.9% R	N E
1986 Turnout	42.5%	32.1%	31.3%
Winner	75.0% R	76.8% R	100.0% R

45

45th

Senate

DISTRICT

House District 89
House District 90

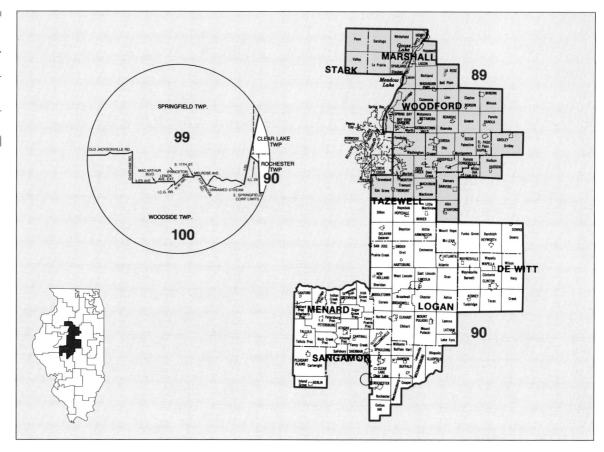

Most of the population of Senate District 45 is rural, non-farm, and over half of its owner-occupied housing is valued under $50,000.

	H.D. 89	H.D. 90	S.D. 45
Voting Age Population	**61,904**	**58,758**	**120,662**
White	99.4%	98.1%	98.8%
Black	.2%	1.3%	.7%
Hispanic	.3%	.4%	.3%
Asian	.1%	.2%	.1%
Age (Total Population)	**96,630**	**96,664**	**193,294**
Under 6	9.8%	8.6%	9.2%
6 to 18	23.1%	20.4%	21.7%
65 and Over	10.2%	12.3%	11.3%
Education (Age 25 and over)	**55,329**	**55,127**	**110,456**
Less than 12 Years	27.1%	32.9%	30.0%
16 Years or More	14.3%	13.6%	14.0%
Urban Population	**44.4%**	**29.0%**	**36.7%**
Family Income (Total Families)	**26,261**	**26,363**	**52,624**
Median Income	$24,148	$21,763	$22,871
Below Poverty Level	1.9%	2.8%	2.4%
With Children Under 6	.8%	1.2%	1.0%
With Children 6 to 17	1.1%	1.9%	1.5%
Headed by Females	.3%	.3%	.3%
Industry (Total Employed)	**42,506**	**43,426**	**85,932**
Professional/Public Admin.	19.7%	29.7%	24.7%
Manufacturing	32.8%	17.1%	24.9%
Retail	15.5%	14.0%	14.7%
Transportation/Communication	5.9%	7.4%	6.7%
Finance/Insurance/Real Estate	5.1%	6.3%	5.7%
Other Service	5.2%	5.9%	5.6%
Housing Units (Total)	**34,586**	**36,371**	**70,957**
Median Value	$54,411	$46,261	$50,336
Owner Occupied	73.4%	68.9%	71.1%
Election Results			
1982 Turnout	57.1%	56.8%	45.1%
Winner	75.8% R	64.6% R	100.0% R
1984 Turnout	57.0%	70.7%	N E
Winner	100.0% R	61.7% R	N E
1986 Turnout	36.0%	44.0%	49.3%
Winner	100.0% R	100.0% R	77.2% R

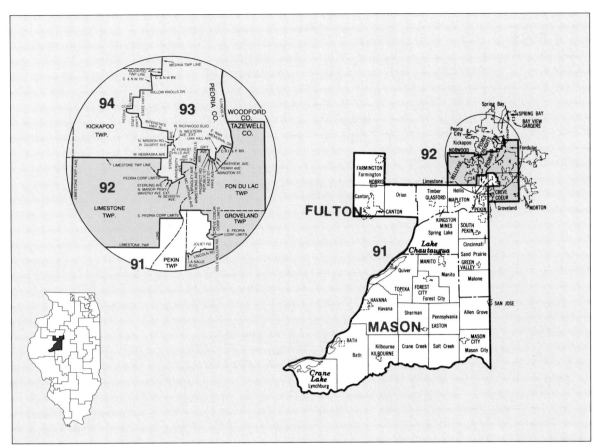

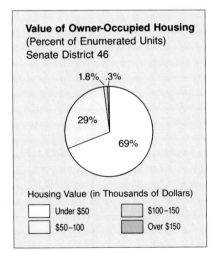

Value of Owner-Occupied Housing
(Percent of Enumerated Units)
Senate District 46

1.8% .3%

29%

69%

Housing Value (in Thousands of Dollars)

☐ Under $50	▨ $100–150
☐ $50–100	▩ Over $150

Senate District 46 ranks in the bottom third among Illinios senate districts in the percentage of college graduates among its population and in the top third in the proportion lacking a high school diploma.

	H.D. 91	H.D. 92	S.D. 46
Voting Age Population	**63,804**	**64,897**	**128,701**
White	99.2%	86.3%	92.7%
Black	.1%	12.6%	6.4%
Hispanic	.4%	.9%	.6%
Asian	.2%	.1%	.2%
Age (Total Population)	**96,492**	**95,993**	**192,485**
Under 6	9.7%	10.5%	10.1%
6 to 18	21.4%	22.1%	21.8%
65 and Over	12.4%	10.2%	11.3%
Education (Age 25 and over)	**56,713**	**52,744**	**109,457**
Less than 12 Years	37.3%	42.2%	39.7%
16 Years or More	8.2%	8.2%	8.2%
Urban Population	**71.0%**	**93.6%**	**82.3%**
Family Income (Total Families)	**26,996**	**24,614**	**51,610**
Median Income	$20,785	$20,279	$20,538
Below Poverty Level	3.3%	4.7%	4.0%
With Children Under 6	1.5%	3.7%	2.6%
With Children 6 to 17	2.3%	3.1%	2.7%
Headed by Females	.6%	2.1%	1.4%
Industry (Total Employed)	**38,592**	**40,229**	**78,821**
Professional/Public Admin.	18.5%	21.9%	20.2%
Manufacturing	31.9%	31.9%	31.9%
Retail	17.5%	17.8%	17.6%
Transportation/Communication	8.5%	7.1%	7.8%
Finance/Insurance/Real Estate	4.9%	4.4%	4.6%
Other Service	5.8%	7.6%	6.7%
Housing Units (Total)	**38,437**	**37,961**	**76,398**
Median Value	$39,754	$39,613	$39,683
Owner Occupied	68.3%	58.2%	63.3%
Election Results			
1982 Turnout	53.2%	44.1%	48.6%
Winner	61.8% D	69.2% D	50.8% D
1984 Turnout	48.8%	40.0%	55.6%
Winner	100.0% D	100.0% D	67.4% D
1986 Turnout	37.6%	27.6%	N E
Winner	72.7% D	69.9% D	N E

47th
Senate
DISTRICT

House District 93
House District 94

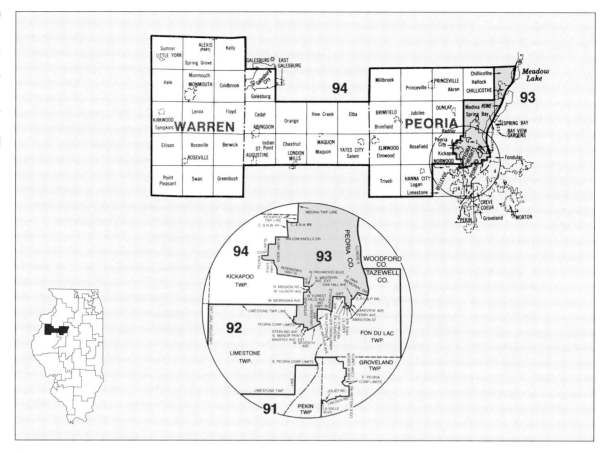

Among the state's house districts, House District 93 ranks in the top third in median value of owner-occupied housing; but House District 94, with two-thirds of its units valued under $50,000, ranks toward the bottom of the middle third.

	H.D. 93	H.D. 94	S.D. 47
Voting Age Population	**67,357**	**64,556**	**131,913**
White	94.5%	95.1%	94.8%
Black	4.3%	3.1%	3.7%
Hispanic	.7%	1.4%	1.0%
Asian	.5%	.3%	.4%
Age (Total Population)	**92,471**	**96,793**	**189,264**
Under 6	8.2%	8.8%	8.5%
6 to 18	19.5%	20.6%	20.1%
65 and Over	11.7%	13.8%	12.8%
Education (Age 25 and over)	**54,692**	**58,051**	**112,743**
Less than 12 Years	21.2%	31.9%	26.7%
16 Years or More	23.6%	12.3%	17.8%
Urban Population	**95.4%**	**61.7%**	**78.1%**
Family Income (Total Families)	**24,668**	**25,810**	**50,478**
Median Income	$26,074	$21,092	$23,305
Below Poverty Level	1.7%	3.3%	2.5%
With Children Under 6	1.0%	1.5%	1.3%
With Children 6 to 17	1.2%	2.1%	1.6%
Headed by Females	.1%	.6%	.4%
Industry (Total Employed)	**44,124**	**41,493**	**85,617**
Professional/Public Admin.	25.9%	24.6%	25.3%
Manufacturing	28.6%	25.7%	27.2%
Retail	18.1%	16.6%	17.4%
Transportation/Communication	5.5%	8.4%	6.9%
Finance/Insurance/Real Estate	6.5%	4.3%	5.5%
Other Service	6.0%	5.3%	5.7%
Housing Units (Total)	**36,520**	**38,220**	**74,740**
Median Value	$53,310	$40,578	$46,944
Owner Occupied	67.2%	65.6%	66.4%
Election Results			
1982 Turnout	56.5%	50.9%	54.4%
Winner	68.9% R	51.2% R	64.3% R
1984 Turnout	50.9%	61.1%	N E
Winner	100.0% R	61.7% R	N E
1986 Turnout	40.7%	45.1%	43.2%
Winner	53.3% R	52.7% R	64.2% R

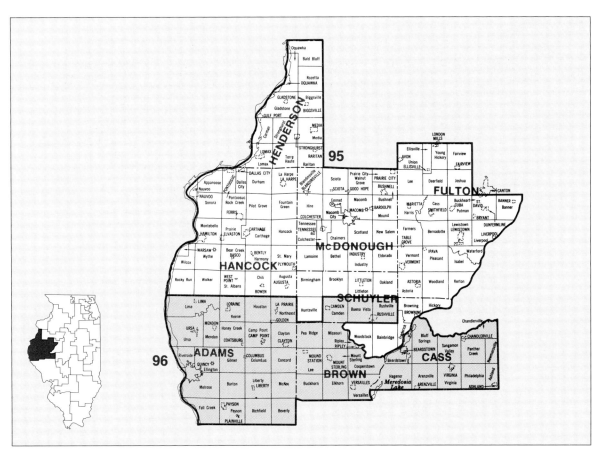

Senate District 48 is a mixed urban and rural non-farm district, in which three-fourths of the owner-occupied housing is valued under $50,000. The district also ranks ninth in the state in the proportion of its population age sixty-five and over.

With Western Illinois University located in House District 95, one-tenth of the district's work force is employed by the state government.

	H.D. 95	H.D. 96	S.D. 48
Voting Age Population	**58,424**	**64,449**	**122,873**
White	97.6%	97.8%	97.7%
Black	1.5%	1.7%	1.6%
Hispanic	.4%	.3%	.4%
Asian	.4%	.1%	.3%
Age (Total Population)	**96,250**	**96,815**	**193,065**
Under 6	8.0%	8.6%	8.3%
6 to 18	20.5%	20.7%	20.6%
65 and Over	13.7%	15.7%	14.7%
Education (Age 25 and over)	**54,051**	**58,657**	**112,708**
Less than 12 Years	32.2%	36.9%	34.6%
16 Years or More	13.2%	10.0%	11.5%
Urban Population	**34.3%**	**54.0%**	**44.1%**
Family Income (Total Families)	**24,833**	**26,010**	**50,843**
Median Income	$18,077	$18,394	$18,244
Below Poverty Level	4.9%	4.3%	4.6%
With Children Under 6	1.7%	1.8%	1.8%
With Children 6 to 17	2.6%	2.7%	2.6%
Headed by Females	.5%	.6%	.6%
Industry (Total Employed)	**39,780**	**40,864**	**80,644**
Professional/Public Admin.	27.0%	24.0%	25.5%
Manufacturing	21.8%	24.9%	23.4%
Retail	15.9%	16.8%	16.4%
Transportation/Communication	5.0%	6.3%	5.7%
Finance/Insurance/Real Estate	3.1%	4.4%	3.8%
Other Service	5.6%	6.7%	6.1%
Housing Units (Total)	**38,531**	**39,133**	**77,664**
Median Value	$31,344	$35,085	$33,214
Owner Occupied	64.3%	67.0%	65.6%
Election Results			
1982 Turnout	40.4%	56.4%	56.1%
Winner	100.0% R	51.3% R	54.9% R
1984 Turnout	64.8%	57.6%	N E
Winner	62.0% R	55.7% R	N E
1986 Turnout	50.0%	51.9%	51.4%
Winner	60.8% R	55.0% R	59.5% R

49

49th
Senate
DISTRICT

House District 97
House District 98

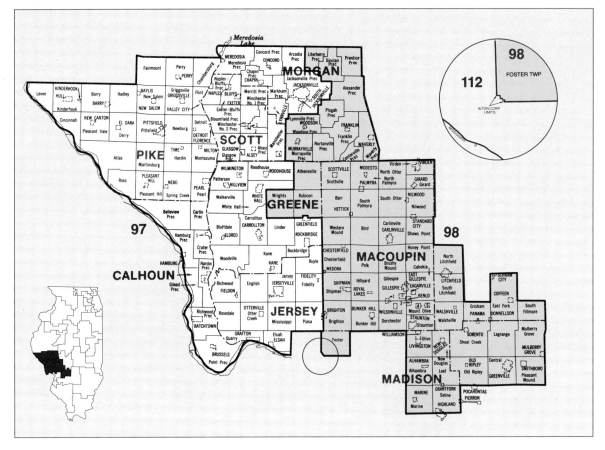

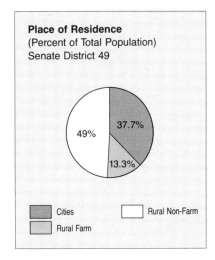

Place of Residence
(Percent of Total Population)
Senate District 49

- Cities
- Rural Farm
- Rural Non-Farm

Senate District 49 ranks eighth in the state in the percentage of population age sixty-five and over.

	H.D. 97	H.D. 98	S.D. 49
Voting Age Population	**58,009**	**60,727**	**118,736**
White	98.3%	99.0%	98.6%
Black	1.2%	.6%	.9%
Hispanic	.4%	.3%	.3%
Asian	.1%	.1%	.1%
Age (Total Population)	**96,997**	**96,639**	**193,636**
Under 6	8.2%	8.6%	8.4%
6 to 18	21.0%	21.0%	21.0%
65 and Over	15.8%	15.7%	15.7%
Education (Age 25 and over)	**58,432**	**58,447**	**116,879**
Less than 12 Years	39.1%	40.7%	39.9%
16 Years or More	10.0%	8.7%	9.3%
Urban Population	**42.4%**	**33.0%**	**37.7%**
Family Income (Total Families)	**26,150**	**26,885**	**53,035**
Median Income	$17,523	$18,919	$18,194
Below Poverty Level	5.1%	4.1%	4.6%
With Children Under 6	1.9%	1.4%	1.6%
With Children 6 to 17	2.6%	2.4%	2.5%
Headed by Females	.6%	.4%	.5%
Industry (Total Employed)	**38,100**	**38,688**	**76,788**
Professional/Public Admin.	27.1%	23.8%	25.4%
Manufacturing	18.5%	21.5%	20.0%
Retail	15.4%	14.7%	15.0%
Transportation/Communication	7.4%	7.6%	7.5%
Finance/Insurance/Real Estate	4.0%	4.2%	4.1%
Other Service	6.2%	5.2%	5.7%
Housing Units (Total)	**39,875**	**38,300**	**78,175**
Median Value	$30,743	$32,295	$31,519
Owner Occupied	64.6%	72.5%	68.5%
Election Results			
1982 Turnout	66.2%	59.6%	62.6%
Winner	60.8% R	57.1% D	62.5% D
1984 Turnout	73.5%	69.6%	51.8%
Winner	53.1% R	60.0% D	100.0% D
1986 Turnout	61.3%	55.7%	N E
Winner	63.5% R	51.8% D	N E

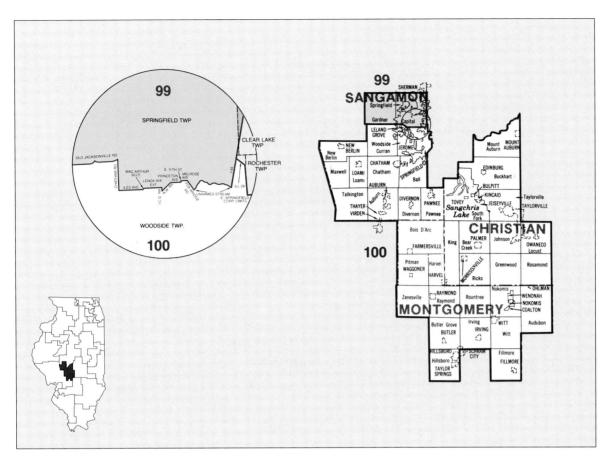

Senate District 50 contains the state capital, and 18.3 percent of its work force is employed by the state government.

	H.D. 99	H.D. 100	S.D. 50
Voting Age Population	**68,147**	**60,416**	**128,563**
White	91.2%	98.5%	94.6%
Black	8.3%	.9%	4.8%
Hispanic	.2%	.3%	.3%
Asian	.2%	.3%	.2%
Age (Total Population)	**95,625**	**94,825**	**190,450**
Under 6	1.3%	6.8%	4.0%
6 to 18	2.9%	17.0%	9.9%
65 and Over	1.4%	11.4%	6.4%
Education (Age 25 and over)	**50,683**	**46,240**	**96,923**
Less than 12 Years	36.6%	36.7%	36.7%
16 Years or More	20.3%	19.0%	19.7%
Urban Population	**95.4%**	**64.1%**	**79.8%**
Family Income (Total Families)	**24,552**	**26,645**	**51,197**
Median Income	$19,865	$21,989	$21,020
Below Poverty Level	3.6%	2.8%	3.2%
With Children Under 6	2.6%	1.0%	1.8%
With Children 6 to 17	2.3%	1.7%	2.0%
Headed by Females	1.3%	.4%	.9%
Industry (Total Employed)	**46,412**	**41,942**	**88,354**
Professional/Public Admin.	44.9%	33.7%	39.6%
Manufacturing	6.7%	12.7%	9.6%
Retail	16.3%	15.9%	16.1%
Transportation/Communication	7.9%	7.8%	7.9%
Finance/Insurance/Real Estate	8.5%	6.8%	7.7%
Other Service	7.5%	5.5%	6.6%
Housing Units (Total)	**42,879**	**37,237**	**80,116**
Median Value	$41,450	$42,857	$42,153
Owner Occupied	55.9%	72.3%	63.5%
Election Results			
1982 Turnout	59.6%	65.4%	62.2%
Winner	51.5% D	62.3% R	63.9% R
1984 Turnout	71.7%	75.7%	N E
Winner	61.6% D	62.7% R	N E
1986 Turnout	59.7%	67.3%	62.7%
Winner	56.0% D	51.9% D	61.3% R

51st
Senate
DISTRICT

House District 101
House District 102

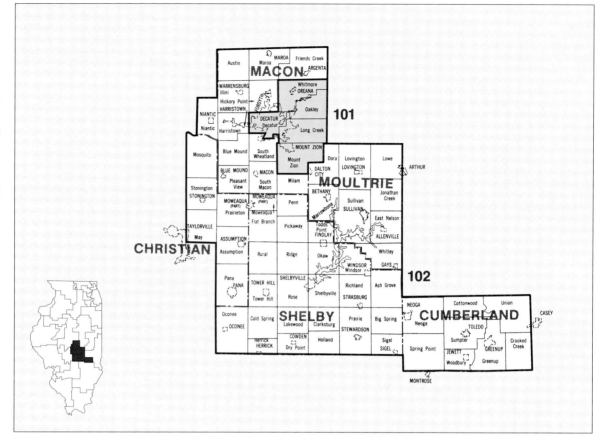

Senate District 51 is a mixed urban and rural district. Nine-tenths of the people in House District 101 live in cities, while half of the population in House District 102 is rural, non-farm.

	H.D. 101	H.D. 102	S.D. 51
Voting Age Population	**68,865**	**54,765**	**123,630**
White	88.4%	98.9%	93.1%
Black	10.8%	.7%	6.3%
Hispanic	.5%	.2%	.4%
Asian	.2%	.1%	.2%
Age (Total Population)	**96,175**	**97,231**	**193,406**
Under 6	9.5%	8.9%	9.2%
6 to 18	20.8%	22.0%	21.4%
65 and Over	12.7%	13.2%	13.0%
Education (Age 25 and over)	**56,307**	**58,221**	**114,528**
Less than 12 Years	34.0%	34.2%	34.1%
16 Years or More	12.7%	10.0%	11.4%
Urban Population	**91.6%**	**36.7%**	**64.0%**
Family Income (Total Families)	**25,918**	**27,172**	**53,090**
Median Income	$21,064	$20,399	$20,718
Below Poverty Level	4.0%	3.1%	3.5%
With Children Under 6	2.6%	1.1%	1.8%
With Children 6 to 17	2.6%	2.0%	2.3%
Headed by Females	1.9%	.4%	1.1%
Industry (Total Employed)	**40,444**	**40,188**	**80,632**
Professional/Public Admin.	24.1%	20.1%	22.1%
Manufacturing	28.9%	25.9%	27.4%
Retail	16.6%	15.5%	16.0%
Transportation/Communication	9.8%	7.7%	8.7%
Finance/Insurance/Real Estate	5.1%	4.7%	4.9%
Other Service	7.3%	5.8%	6.6%
Housing Units (Total)	**38,359**	**38,047**	**76,406**
Median Value	$38,235	$38,034	$38,134
Owner Occupied	66.8%	70.9%	68.9%
Election Results			
1982 Turnout	44.6%	65.9%	53.9%
Winner	66.5% D	52.5% R	55.7% R
1984 Turnout	54.7%	78.3%	N E
Winner	63.9% D	58.5% R	N E
1986 Turnout	37.3%	45.3%	47.9%
Winner	72.3% D	100.0% R	53.4% D

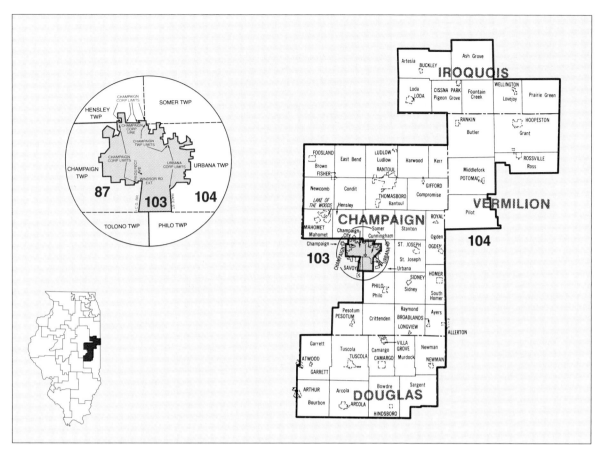

Senate District 52 contains the University of Illinois, and 30.2 percent of the work force of House District 103 is employed by the state government.

	H.D. 103	H.D. 104	S.D. 52
Voting Age Population	**73,442**	**59,866**	**133,288**
White	87.6%	94.8%	90.8%
Black	8.8%	3.1%	6.3%
Hispanic	1.0%	1.4%	1.2%
Asian	2.5%	.6%	1.6%
Age (Total Population)	**95,652**	**97,785**	**193,437**
Under 6	5.8%	9.8%	7.8%
6 to 18	16.1%	22.2%	19.2%
65 and Over	7.3%	9.4%	8.4%
Education (Age 25 and over)	**43,595**	**53,370**	**96,965**
Less than 12 Years	16.8%	27.3%	22.6%
16 Years or More	38.0%	12.2%	23.8%
Urban Population	**99.5%**	**44.4%**	**71.6%**
Family Income (Total Families)	**18,090**	**26,066**	**44,156**
Median Income	$21,025	$20,221	$20,533
Below Poverty Level	4.0%	2.9%	3.3%
With Children Under 6	2.0%	1.8%	1.9%
With Children 6 to 17	1.6%	1.9%	1.8%
Headed by Females	1.2%	.6%	.8%
Industry (Total Employed)	**45,183**	**38,936**	**84,119**
Professional/Public Admin.	50.0%	24.8%	38.4%
Manufacturing	8.3%	19.0%	13.3%
Retail	18.3%	17.2%	17.8%
Transportation/Communication	5.2%	7.6%	6.3%
Finance/Insurance/Real Estate	3.8%	4.4%	4.1%
Other Service	6.9%	6.7%	6.8%
Housing Units (Total)	**35,925**	**36,922**	**72,847**
Median Value	$49,705	$41,122	$45,413
Owner Occupied	43.7%	62.8%	53.4%
Election Results			
1982 Turnout	37.4%	47.2%	41.3%
Winner	60.9% D	68.9% R	60.4% R
1984 Turnout	54.6%	49.1%	55.6%
Winner	62.2% D	100.0% R	66.9% R
1986 Turnout	28.9%	44.7%	N E
Winner	61.2% D	70.9% R	N E

53rd

Senate
DISTRICT

House District 105
House District 106

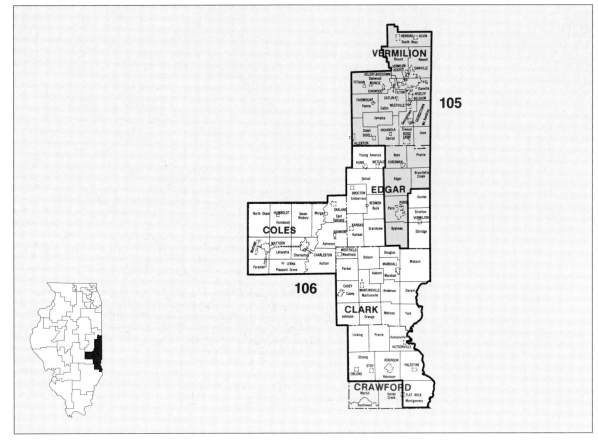

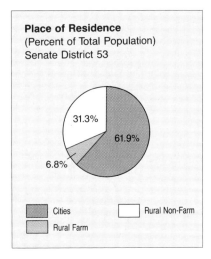

Place of Residence
(Percent of Total Population)
Senate District 53

61.9%
31.3%
6.8%

- Cities
- Rural Farm
- Rural Non-Farm

Over three-quarters of the owner-occupied housing in Senate District 53 is valued under $50,000, ranking the district in the bottom third in median value of its housing units.

	H.D. 105	H.D. 106	S.D. 53
Voting Age Population	67,376	67,023	134,399
White	92.8%	98.3%	95.5%
Black	6.0%	1.2%	3.6%
Hispanic	.8%	.3%	.5%
Asian	.3%	.2%	.3%
Age (Total Population)	96,516	95,337	191,853
Under 6	9.2%	7.9%	8.6%
6 to 18	20.8%	19.1%	19.9%
65 and Over	13.8%	14.3%	14.0%
Education (Age 25 and over)	58,195	54,616	112,811
Less than 12 Years	37.9%	35.3%	36.6%
16 Years or More	9.9%	12.7%	11.2%
Urban Population	**68.7%**	**54.9%**	**61.9%**
Family Income (Total Families)	26,355	24,803	51,158
Median Income	$18,743	$18,773	$18,757
Below Poverty Level	4.5%	3.5%	4.0%
With Children Under 6	2.0%	1.5%	1.8%
With Children 6 to 17	2.7%	2.1%	2.5%
Headed by Females	1.3%	.4%	.8%
Industry (Total Employed)	38,938	39,948	78,886
Professional/Public Admin.	23.0%	24.8%	23.9%
Manufacturing	30.6%	23.8%	27.1%
Retail	17.2%	17.4%	17.3%
Transportation/Communication	6.7%	6.5%	6.6%
Finance/Insurance/Real Estate	4.0%	3.4%	3.7%
Other Service	6.0%	5.5%	5.8%
Housing Units (Total)	39,008	38,224	77,232
Median Value	$32,852	$32,798	$32,825
Owner Occupied	66.9%	66.3%	66.6%
Election Results			
1982 Turnout	48.5%	50.6%	49.2%
Winner	54.3% D	62.3% R	58.3% R
1984 Turnout	60.0%	57.6%	N E
Winner	54.2% R	55.3% R	N E
1986 Turnout	43.7%	46.0%	44.9%
Winner	52.5% R	70.2% R	63.7% R

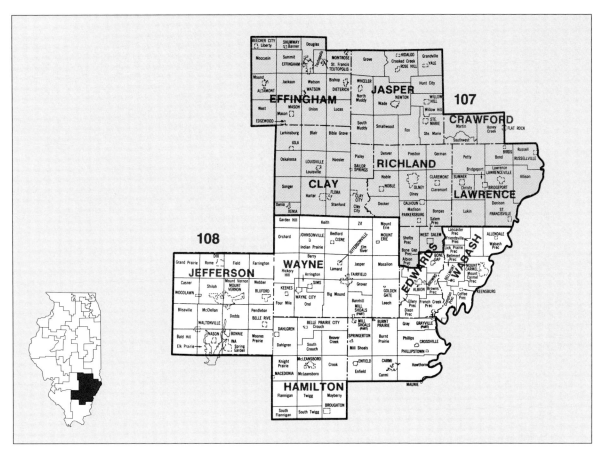

House District 107
House District 108

Place of Residence
(Percent of Total Population)
Senate District 54

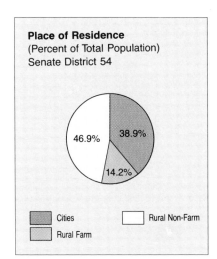

46.9%   38.9%
14.2%

☐ Cities   ☐ Rural Non-Farm
☐ Rural Farm

Senate District 54 ranks in the bottom third in median value of owner-occupied housing, with three-fourths of its units valued under $50,000.

	H.D. 107	H.D. 108	S.D. 54
Voting Age Population	**58,012**	**62,503**	**120,515**
White	99.5%	98.1%	98.8%
Black	.2%	1.5%	.8%
Hispanic	.2%	.2%	.2%
Asian	.1%	.1%	.1%
Age (Total Population)	**97,445**	**97,348**	**194,793**
Under 6	9.2%	8.5%	8.8%
6 to 18	21.1%	19.7%	20.4%
65 and Over	15.7%	16.8%	16.3%
Education (Age 25 and over)	**58,336**	**60,777**	**119,113**
Less than 12 Years	41.0%	44.8%	43.0%
16 Years or More	8.3%	8.6%	8.4%
Urban Population	**35.4%**	**42.4%**	**38.9%**
Family Income (Total Families)	**26,948**	**27,814**	**54,762**
Median Income	$17,661	$17,074	$17,344
Below Poverty Level	4.6%	5.3%	4.9%
With Children Under 6	1.5%	1.7%	1.6%
With Children 6 to 17	2.3%	2.8%	2.5%
Headed by Females	.3%	.7%	.5%
Industry (Total Employed)	**38,845**	**38,603**	**77,448**
Professional/Public Admin.	20.7%	22.5%	21.6%
Manufacturing	21.7%	18.1%	19.9%
Retail	16.3%	16.4%	16.3%
Transportation/Communication	7.1%	6.8%	6.9%
Finance/Insurance/Real Estate	4.2%	4.6%	4.4%
Other Service	6.1%	6.7%	6.4%
Housing Units (Total)	**39,163**	**41,704**	**80,867**
Median Value	$32,134	$30,148	$31,141
Owner Occupied	71.3%	69.2%	70.2%
Election Results			
1982 Turnout	61.1%	62.1%	61.7%
Winner	54.7% D	50.1% D	63.8% D
1984 Turnout	49.8%	72.1%	N E
Winner	100.0% D	53.5% D	N E
1986 Turnout	61.2%	58.2%	60.1%
Winner	67.5% D	65.3% D	57.4% D

55th
Senate
DISTRICT

House District 109
House District 110

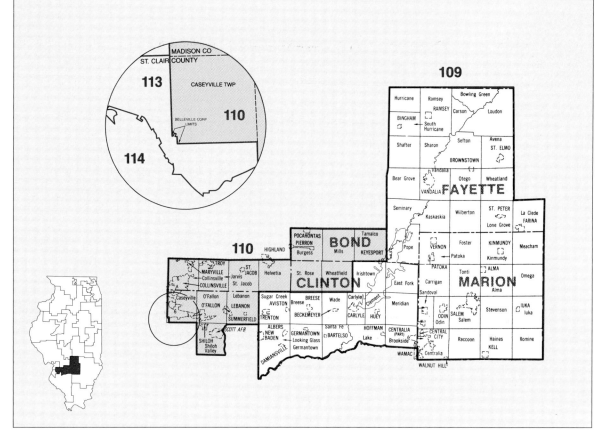

Senate District 55 is a mixed urban and rural district. While 77.8 percent of the population of House District 110 lives in cities, half of the people in House District 109 are rural, non-farm.

	H.D. 109	H.D. 110	S.D. 55
Voting Age Population	**62,099**	**70,407**	**132,506**
White	97.1%	95.6%	96.3%
Black	2.2%	2.4%	2.3%
Hispanic	.5%	1.1%	.8%
Asian	.2%	.7%	.5%
Age (Total Population)	**96,468**	**99,151**	**195,619**
Under 6	9.1%	8.7%	8.9%
6 to 18	21.5%	22.5%	22.0%
65 and Over	14.9%	10.1%	12.5%
Education (Age 25 and over)	**57,056**	**57,855**	**114,911**
Less than 12 Years	44.8%	31.9%	38.2%
16 Years or More	7.6%	13.8%	10.7%
Urban Population	**39.1%**	**77.8%**	**58.7%**
Family Income (Total Families)	**26,173**	**27,035**	**53,208**
Median Income	$18,013	$22,281	$20,196
Below Poverty Level	4.2%	1.8%	3.0%
With Children Under 6	1.7%	1.1%	1.4%
With Children 6 to 17	2.8%	1.9%	2.3%
Headed by Females	.7%	.4%	.6%
Industry (Total Employed)	**37,837**	**39,839**	**77,676**
Professional/Public Admin.	22.2%	24.7%	23.5%
Manufacturing	20.9%	19.2%	20.0%
Retail	15.8%	19.2%	17.6%
Transportation/Communication	9.8%	9.5%	9.6%
Finance/Insurance/Real Estate	4.4%	6.8%	5.6%
Other Service	6.6%	7.1%	6.9%
Housing Units (Total)	**38,061**	**35,448**	**73,509**
Median Value	$31,851	$46,049	$38,950
Owner Occupied	70.7%	69.7%	70.2%
Election Results			
1982 Turnout	52.0%	34.4%	42.9%
Winner	53.7% R	53.2% D	58.1% R
1984 Turnout	66.9%	56.9%	61.6%
Winner	54.1% R	54.3% R	63.7% R
1986 Turnout	55.8%	35.8%	N E
Winner	53.0% D	61.3% R	N E

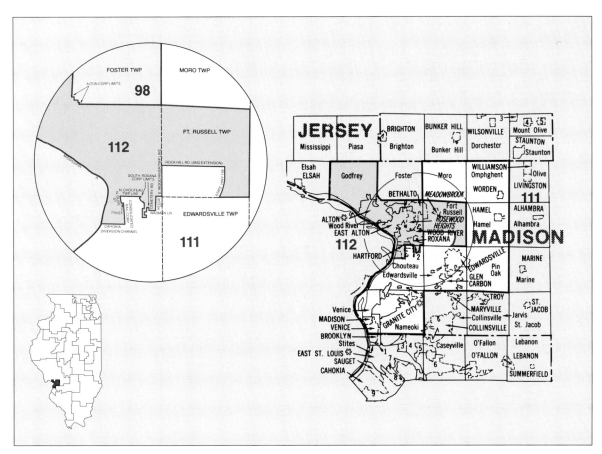

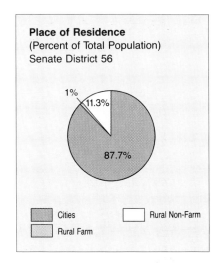

Place of Residence
(Percent of Total Population)
Senate District 56

- Cities
- Rural Non-Farm
- Rural Farm

1%
11.3%
87.7%

Southern Illinois University at Edwardsville is in House District 111, and 5.8 percent of the district's workers are employed by the state government.

	H.D. 111	H.D. 112	S.D. 56
Voting Age Population	68,246	65,871	134,117
White	93.0%	91.9%	92.4%
Black	5.5%	7.0%	6.2%
Hispanic	.9%	.8%	.9%
Asian	.4%	.2%	.3%
Age (Total Population)	96,049	95,631	191,680
Under 6	8.4%	8.4%	8.4%
6 to 18	21.9%	21.6%	21.7%
65 and Over	10.7%	12.6%	11.7%
Education (Age 25 and over)	55,785	56,739	112,524
Less than 12 Years	39.0%	36.4%	37.7%
16 Years or More	12.2%	9.4%	10.8%
Urban Population	82.4%	93.0%	87.7%
Family Income (Total Families)	26,015	26,175	52,190
Median Income	$21,533	$20,383	$20,949
Below Poverty Level	3.4%	3.4%	3.4%
With Children Under 6	2.1%	2.0%	2.0%
With Children 6 to 17	2.6%	3.2%	2.9%
Headed by Females	1.0%	1.3%	1.2%
Industry (Total Employed)	40,404	37,293	77,697
Professional/Public Admin.	27.2%	25.9%	26.6%
Manufacturing	27.5%	31.2%	29.3%
Retail	14.9%	17.1%	15.9%
Transportation/Communication	8.8%	6.5%	7.7%
Finance/Insurance/Real Estate	6.1%	5.1%	5.6%
Other Service	6.1%	6.4%	6.2%
Housing Units (Total)	36,017	36,750	72,767
Median Value	$36,170	$32,452	$34,311
Owner Occupied	68.9%	70.5%	69.7%
Election Results			
1982 Turnout	29.7%	39.2%	37.4%
Winner	100.0% D	57.7% D	75.7% D
1984 Turnout	45.5%	41.5%	N E
Winner	100.0% D	100.0% D	N E
1986 Turnout	33.7%	25.9%	27.6%
Winner	70.0% D	100.0% D	100.0% D

57th
Senate
DISTRICT

House District 113
House District 114

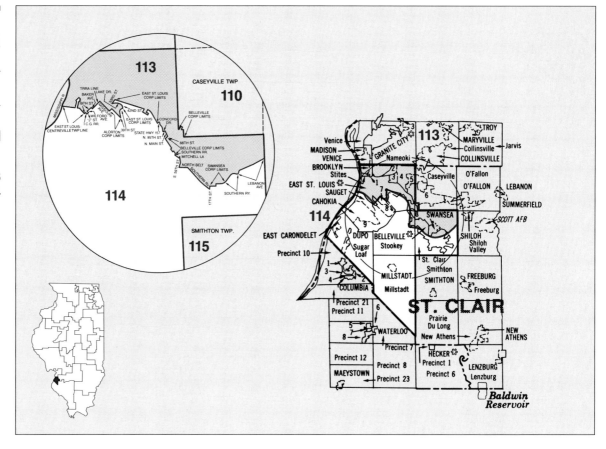

Senate District 57 ranks in the bottom third in median income and median value of owner-occupied housing, and in the top third in the percentage of population falling below the poverty line.

In House District 113, 10.4 percent of the work force is employed by local government, the second-highest percentage in the state outside Chicago.

	H.D. 113	H.D. 114	S.D. 57
Voting Age Population	**56,065**	**62,643**	**118,708**
White	50.7%	85.6%	69.1%
Black	48.0%	13.6%	29.8%
Hispanic	1.2%	.5%	.8%
Asian	.1%	.2%	.1%
Age (Total Population)	**96,142**	**97,272**	**193,414**
Under 6	8.5%	7.2%	7.9%
6 to 18	20.7%	18.0%	19.3%
65 and Over	9.6%	8.9%	9.2%
Education (Age 25 and over)	**39,794**	**42,925**	**82,719**
Less than 12 Years	62.1%	51.8%	56.8%
16 Years or More	11.6%	15.6%	13.7%
Urban Population	**96.5%**	**88.9%**	**92.6%**
Family Income (Total Families)	**23,170**	**25,647**	**48,817**
Median Income	$15,019	$20,454	$17,990
Below Poverty Level	12.0%	4.6%	8.1%
With Children Under 6	4.4%	2.1%	3.2%
With Children 6 to 17	9.0%	3.6%	6.2%
Headed by Females	6.5%	1.5%	3.9%
Industry (Total Employed)	**29,617**	**38,709**	**68,326**
Professional/Public Admin.	32.5%	27.7%	29.8%
Manufacturing	19.7%	19.7%	19.7%
Retail	15.8%	17.0%	16.5%
Transportation/Communication	10.3%	11.3%	10.8%
Finance/Insurance/Real Estate	5.7%	6.2%	6.0%
Other Service	7.2%	7.2%	7.2%
Housing Units (Total)	**35,693**	**35,827**	**71,520**
Median Value	$24,437	$34,362	$29,399
Owner Occupied	53.4%	66.8%	60.1%
Election Results			
1982 Turnout	48.0%	30.4%	46.0%
Winner	76.6% D	100.0% D	59.4% D
1984 Turnout	61.8%	54.7%	N E
Winner	72.8% D	61.5% D	N E
1986 Turnout	34.0%	36.6%	28.0%
Winner	70.9% D	59.2% D	100.0% D

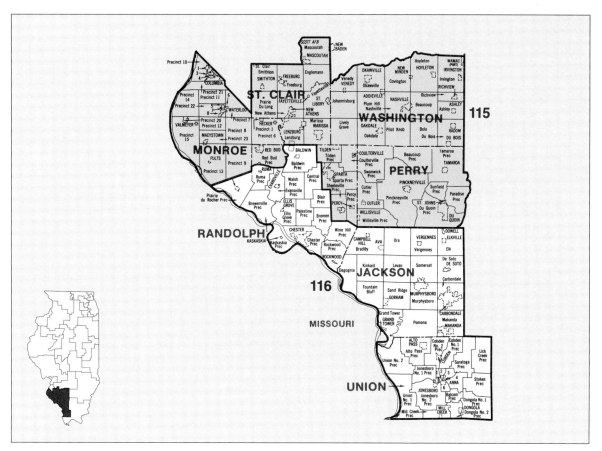

House District 115
House District 116

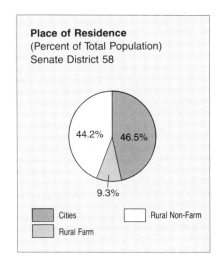

Place of Residence
(Percent of Total Population)
Senate District 58

44.2%   46.5%

9.3%

Cities   Rural Non-Farm

Rural Farm

Senate District 58 ranks in the bottom third in median income and median value of owner-occupied housing, and in the top third in percentage of population below the poverty level.

Southern Illinois University at Carbondale is in House District 116, and 24.3 percent of that district's workers are employed by the state government.

	H.D. 115	H.D. 116	S.D. 58
Voting Age Population	59,555	68,937	128,492
White	98.3%	90.2%	94.0%
Black	1.4%	8.0%	5.0%
Hispanic	.3%	.9%	.6%
Asian	.0%	.8%	.4%
Age (Total Population)	96,967	97,440	194,407
Under 6	8.9%	6.9%	7.9%
6 to 18	21.3%	17.7%	19.5%
65 and Over	14.8%	12.3%	13.6%
Education (Age 25 and over)	58,367	52,969	111,336
Less than 12 Years	43.9%	38.1%	41.2%
16 Years or More	7.9%	17.8%	12.6%
Urban Population	41.7%	51.3%	46.5%
Family Income (Total Families)	26,694	22,555	49,249
Median Income	$21,067	$17,732	$19,541
Below Poverty Level	3.5%	6.3%	4.8%
With Children Under 6	1.1%	1.6%	1.3%
With Children 6 to 17	2.1%	2.7%	2.4%
Headed by Females	.4%	.9%	.6%
Industry (Total Employed)	38,426	38,667	77,093
Professional/Public Admin.	21.7%	41.6%	31.7%
Manufacturing	18.4%	11.7%	15.1%
Retail	14.2%	16.0%	15.1%
Transportation/Communication	8.5%	6.5%	7.5%
Finance/Insurance/Real Estate	4.8%	3.7%	4.2%
Other Service	4.9%	5.9%	5.4%
Housing Units (Total)	37,985	37,495	75,480
Median Value	$38,218	$34,968	$36,593
Owner Occupied	72.2%	58.1%	65.2%
Election Results			
1982 Turnout	59.3%	46.5%	53.2%
Winner	63.0% R	66.4% D	56.5% D
1984 Turnout	73.9%	42.3%	67.1%
Winner	55.5% R	100.0% D	52.7% R
1986 Turnout	58.7%	42.7%	N E
Winner	56.3% R	68.6% D	N E

House District 117
House District 118

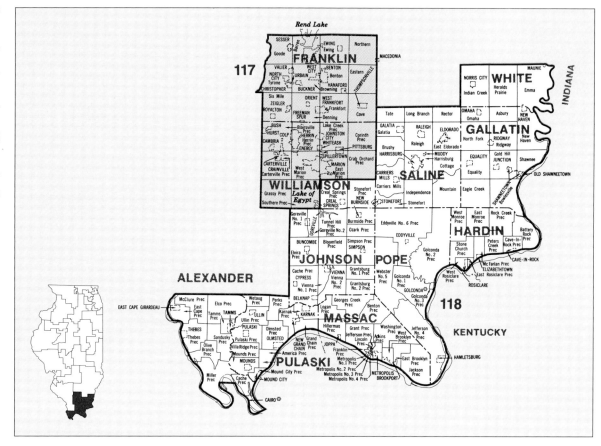

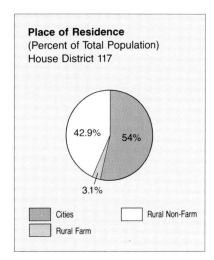

Place of Residence
(Percent of Total Population)
House District 117

42.9%   54%   3.1%

Cities | Rural Non-Farm
Rural Farm

Senate District 59 ranks second in the state in the percentage of population age sixty-five and over.

House District 118 is 70.8 percent rural, mostly non-farm, and it has a higher percentage of owner-occupied housing valued under $50,000 (87.4%) and workers employed by local government (10.7%) than any district outside Chicago.

	H.D. 117	H.D. 118	S.D. 59
Voting Age Population	**69,369**	**61,137**	**130,506**
White	98.5%	91.5%	95.2%
Black	.9%	8.1%	4.3%
Hispanic	.4%	.3%	.4%
Asian	.2%	.1%	.1%
Age (Total Population)	**96,750**	**98,255**	**195,005**
Under 6	8.0%	8.2%	8.1%
6 to 18	19.8%	20.2%	20.0%
65 and Over	16.6%	17.9%	17.3%
Education (Age 25 and over)	**61,068**	**61,614**	**122,682**
Less than 12 Years	44.1%	50.3%	47.2%
16 Years or More	8.9%	6.9%	7.9%
Urban Population	**54.0%**	**29.2%**	**41.5%**
Family Income (Total Families)	**27,319**	**27,387**	**54,706**
Median Income	$17,320	$15,187	$16,179
Below Poverty Level	4.7%	7.3%	6.0%
With Children Under 6	2.0%	2.2%	2.1%
With Children 6 to 17	3.4%	4.3%	3.8%
Headed by Females	.6%	1.2%	.9%
Industry (Total Employed)	**34,720**	**32,946**	**67,666**
Professional/Public Admin.	24.9%	28.5%	26.7%
Manufacturing	14.1%	11.9%	13.1%
Retail	16.9%	15.7%	16.3%
Transportation/Communication	6.8%	8.6%	7.7%
Finance/Insurance/Real Estate	4.0%	3.3%	3.7%
Other Service	6.9%	5.5%	6.2%
Housing Units (Total)	**41,936**	**42,208**	**84,144**
Median Value	$27,404	$24,187	$25,795
Owner Occupied	69.1%	67.9%	68.5%
Election Results			
1982 Turnout	52.6%	67.5%	59.7%
Winner	65.0% D	50.3% R	53.6% D
1984 Turnout	64.0%	75.8%	70.7%
Winner	69.6% D	55.3% D	51.2% D
1986 Turnout	53.6%	65.9%	59.0%
Winner	69.3% D	58.0% D	71.6% D

Legislative
SUMMARY
MAPS

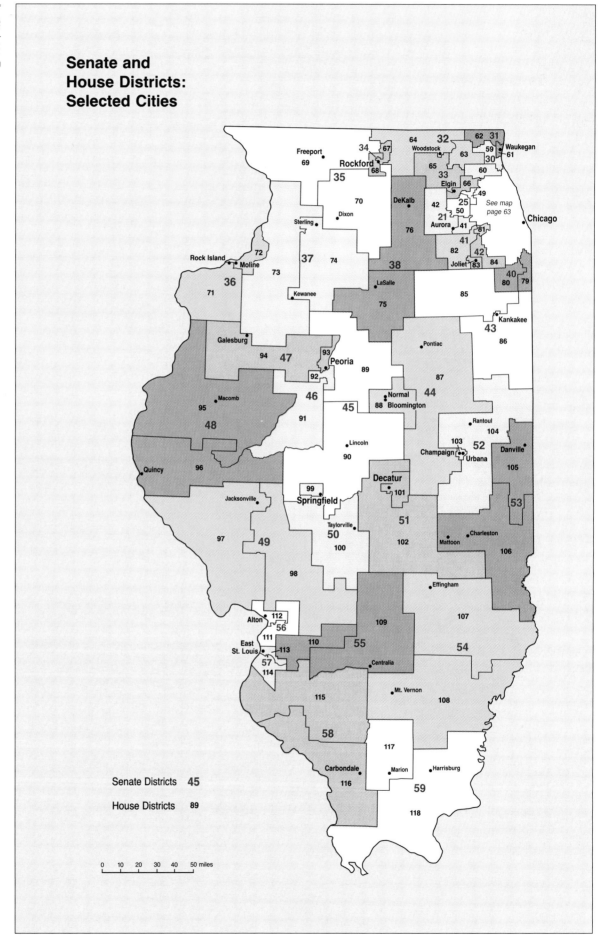

**Senate and
House Districts:
Selected Cities**

Senate Districts 45

House Districts 89

0 10 20 30 40 50 miles

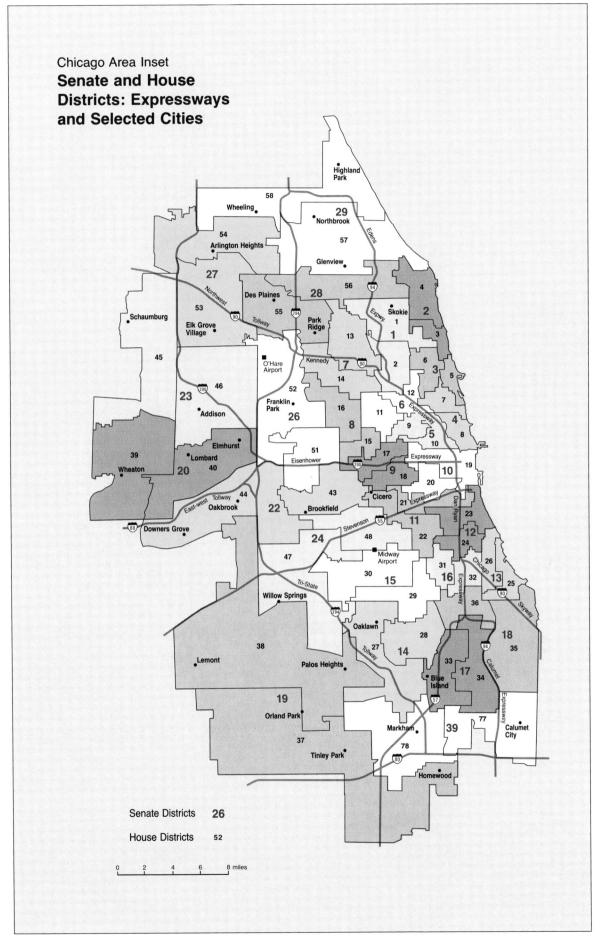

Chicago Area Inset
**Senate and House
Districts: Expressways
and Selected Cities**

Highland
Park

58

Wheeling

29
Northbrook

54
Arlington Heights

57

27

Glenview

56

Des Plaines
28

Schaumburg

53

55

Elk Grove
Village

294

Park
Ridge

13

94

Skokie
1

4

2

1

3

45

O'Hare
Airport

Kennedy

290

7

80

2

6

3

5

46

23

52

14

12

7

Addison

Franklin
Park

26

16

11

6

Expressway

4

8

Elmhurst

8

9

5

Lombard

39

51

15

10

Wheaton

20

40

Eisenhower

290

17

Expressway

19

10

9

18

20

22

43

Oakbrook

Cicero

21

Expressway

10

88

Downers Grove

24

Brookfield

Stevenson

55

11

22

23

Dan Ryan

12

24

47

48

Midway
Airport

31

16

26

Chicago

13

25

Tri-State

30

15

29

32

36

90

Skyway

294

Willow Springs

Oaklawn

28

Tollway

38

27

14

33

94

18

35

Lemont

Palos Heights

17

34

Calumet

19

57

Orland Park

Markham

39

77

Calumet
City

37

78

Tinley Park

80

Blue
Island

Homewood

Senate Districts **26**

House Districts   **52**

0   2   4   6   8 miles

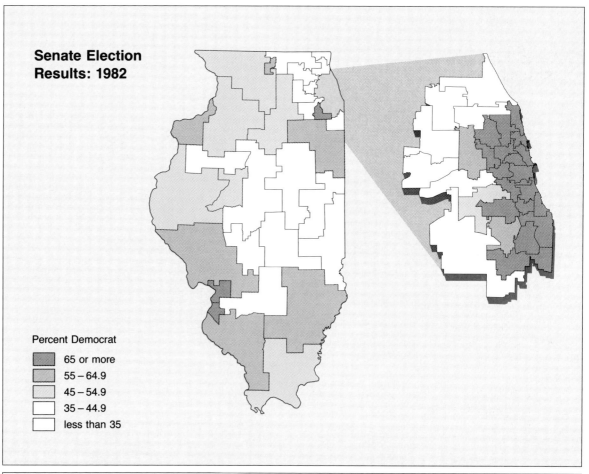

**Senate Election
Results: 1982**

Percent Democrat

- 65 or more
- 55 – 64.9
- 45 – 54.9
- 35 – 44.9
- less than 35

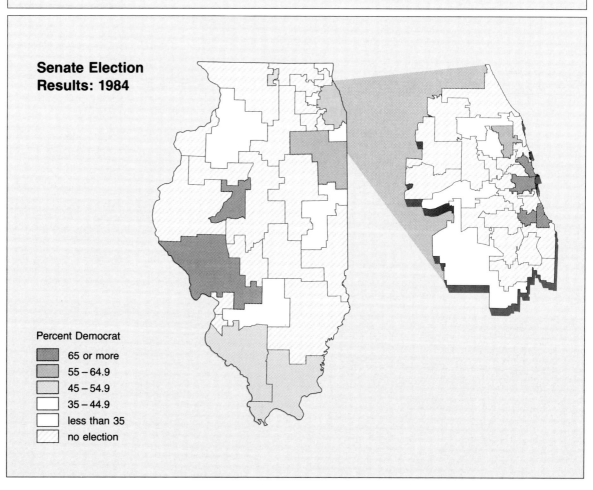

**Senate Election
Results: 1984**

Percent Democrat

- 65 or more
- 55 – 64.9
- 45 – 54.9
- 35 – 44.9
- less than 35
- no election

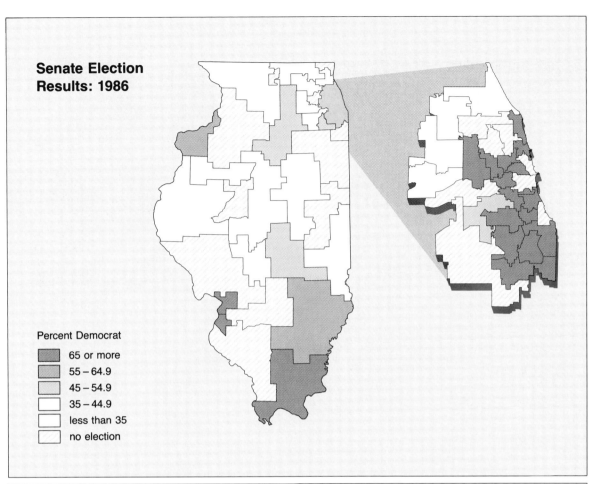

**Senate Election
Results: 1986**

Percent Democrat

- 65 or more
- 55 – 64.9
- 45 – 54.9
- 35 – 44.9
- less than 35
- no election

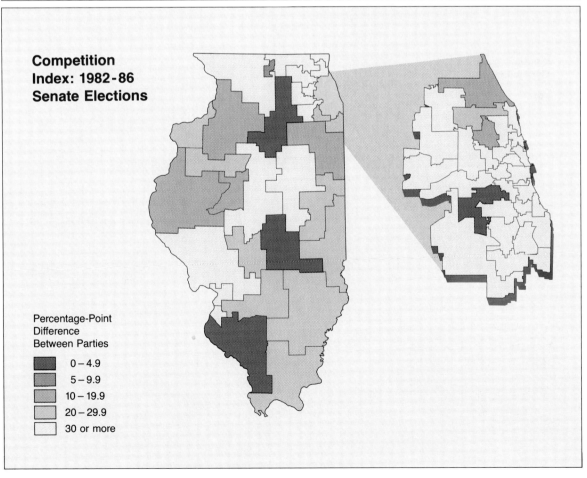

**Competition
Index: 1982-86
Senate Elections**

Percentage-Point
Difference
Between Parties

- 0 – 4.9
- 5 – 9.9
- 10 – 19.9
- 20 – 29.9
- 30 or more

65

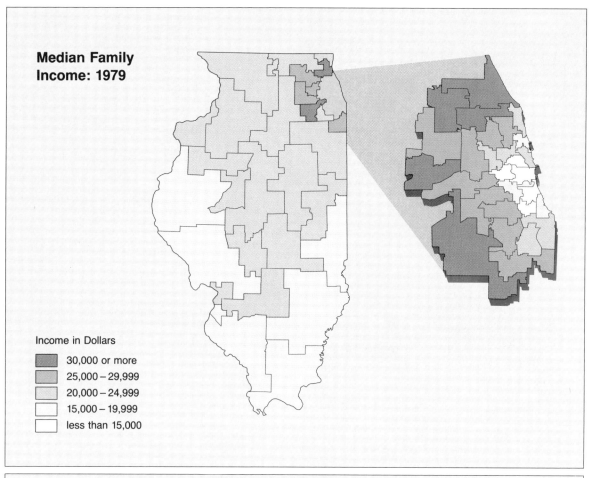

**Median Family
Income: 1979**

Income in Dollars

- 30,000 or more
- 25,000 – 29,999
- 20,000 – 24,999
- 15,000 – 19,999
- less than 15,000

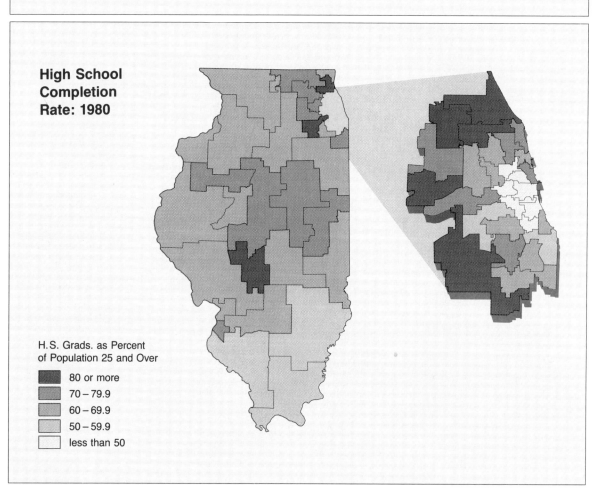

**High School
Completion
Rate: 1980**

H.S. Grads. as Percent
of Population 25 and Over

- 80 or more
- 70 – 79.9
- 60 – 69.9
- 50 – 59.9
- less than 50

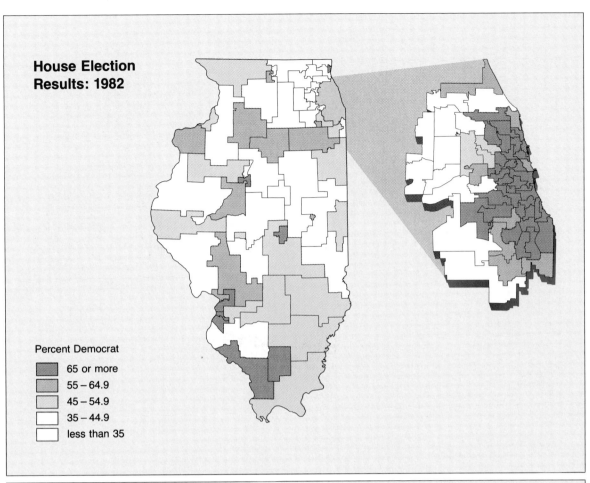

**House Election
Results: 1982**

Percent Democrat

- 65 or more
- 55 – 64.9
- 45 – 54.9
- 35 – 44.9
- less than 35

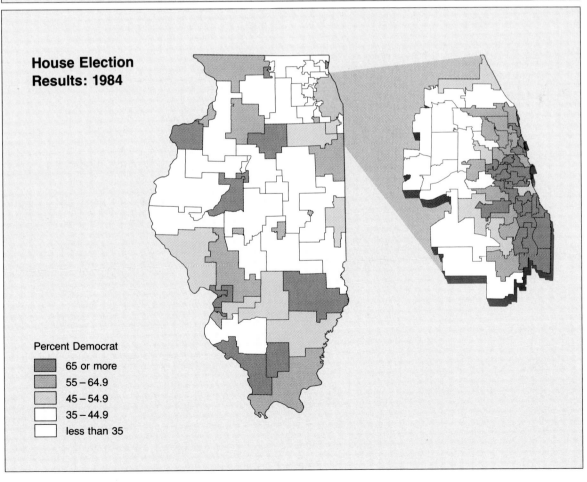

**House Election
Results: 1984**

Percent Democrat

- 65 or more
- 55 – 64.9
- 45 – 54.9
- 35 – 44.9
- less than 35

67

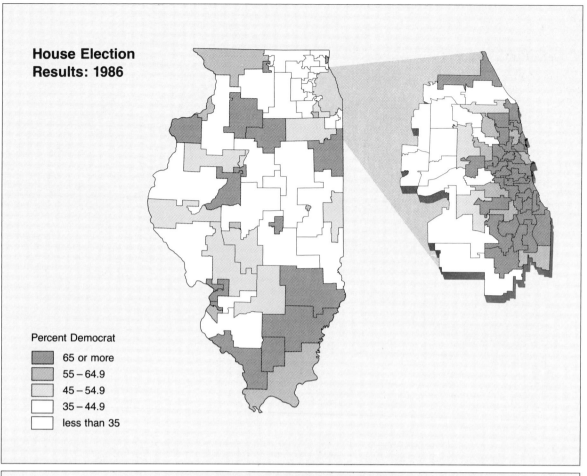

**House Election
Results: 1986**

Percent Democrat

- 65 or more
- 55 – 64.9
- 45 – 54.9
- 35 – 44.9
- less than 35

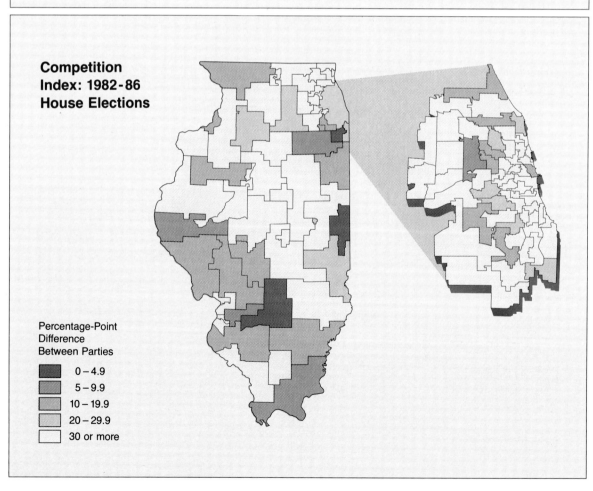

**Competition
Index: 1982-86
House Elections**

Percentage-Point
Difference
Between Parties

- 0 – 4.9
- 5 – 9.9
- 10 – 19.9
- 20 – 29.9
- 30 or more

**Median Family
Income: 1979**

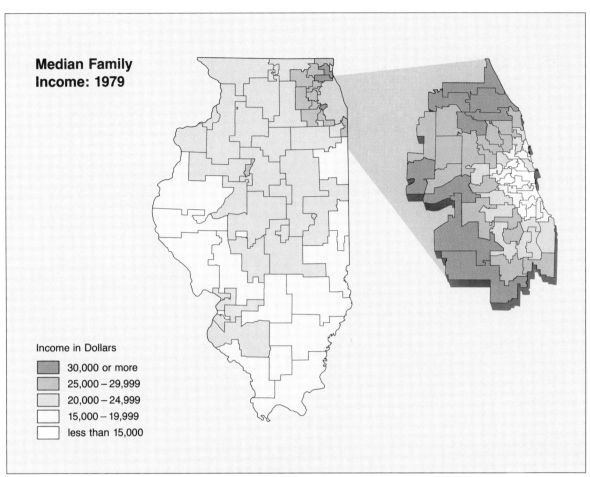

Income in Dollars

- 30,000 or more
- 25,000 – 29,999
- 20,000 – 24,999
- 15,000 – 19,999
- less than 15,000

**High School
Completion
Rate: 1980**

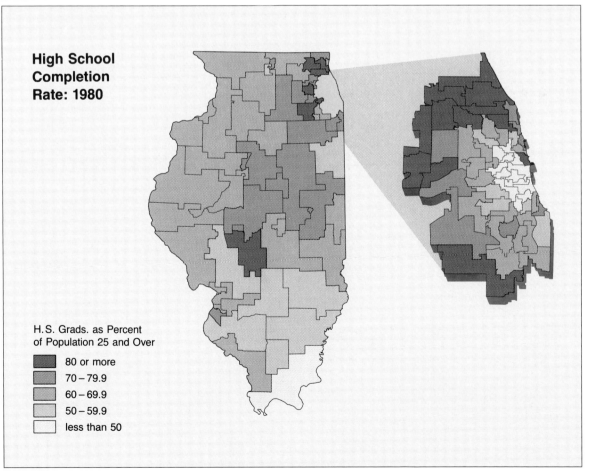

H.S. Grads. as Percent
of Population 25 and Over

- 80 or more
- 70 – 79.9
- 60 – 69.9
- 50 – 59.9
- less than 50

69

★ County ★
SUMMARY
MAPS

**Counties and
Selected Cities**

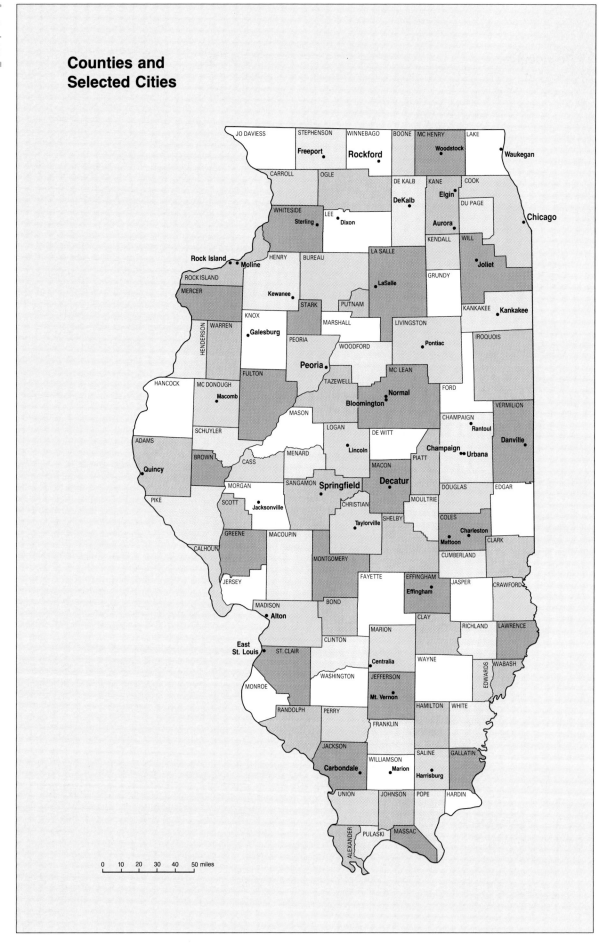

JO DAVIESS | STEPHENSON | WINNEBAGO | BOONE | MC HENRY | LAKE

Freeport | Rockford | Woodstock | Waukegan

CARROLL | OGLE | DE KALB | KANE | COOK

WHITESIDE | Elgin | DU PAGE | Chicago

Sterling | LEE | DeKalb | Aurora

Dixon | KENDALL | WILL

Rock Island | HENRY | BUREAU | LA SALLE | Joliet

Moline | LaSalle | GRUNDY

ROCK ISLAND | KANKAKEE

MERCER | Kewanee | STARK | PUTNAM | Kankakee

KNOX | MARSHALL | LIVINGSTON | IROQUOIS

WARREN | Galesburg | PEORIA | WOODFORD | Pontiac

HENDERSON | Peoria | MC LEAN

FULTON | TAZEWELL | FORD

HANCOCK | MC DONOUGH | Normal | CHAMPAIGN | VERMILION

Macomb | Bloomington | Rantoul

MASON | LOGAN | DE WITT | Danville

SCHUYLER | Lincoln | Champaign

ADAMS | MACON | PIATT | Urbana

BROWN | MENARD | Decatur | DOUGLAS | EDGAR

Quincy | CASS | SANGAMON | MOULTRIE

MORGAN | Springfield | COLES

PIKE | SCOTT | Jacksonville | CHRISTIAN | Charleston | CLARK

Taylorville | SHELBY | Mattoon

GREENE | MACOUPIN | CUMBERLAND

CALHOUN | MONTGOMERY | FAYETTE | EFFINGHAM | JASPER | CRAWFORD

JERSEY | Effingham

MADISON | BOND | CLAY | RICHLAND | LAWRENCE

Alton | MARION | EDWARDS | WABASH

CLINTON | Centralia | WAYNE

East St. Louis | ST. CLAIR | JEFFERSON

MONROE | WASHINGTON | Mt. Vernon | HAMILTON | WHITE

RANDOLPH | PERRY | FRANKLIN

JACKSON | WILLIAMSON | SALINE | GALLATIN

Carbondale | Marion | Harrisburg

UNION | JOHNSON | POPE | HARDIN

ALEXANDER | PULASKI | MASSAC

0 10 20 30 40   50 miles

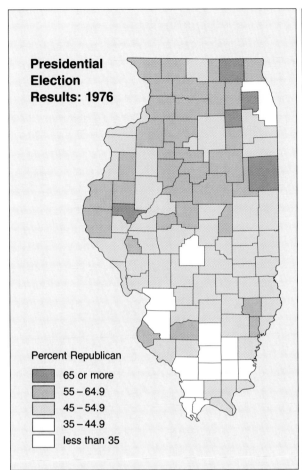

**Presidential
Election
Results: 1976**

Percent Republican

- 65 or more
- 55 – 64.9
- 45 – 54.9
- 35 – 44.9
- less than 35

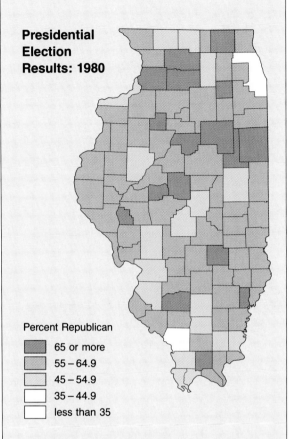

**Presidential
Election
Results: 1980**

Percent Republican

- 65 or more
- 55 – 64.9
- 45 – 54.9
- 35 – 44.9
- less than 35

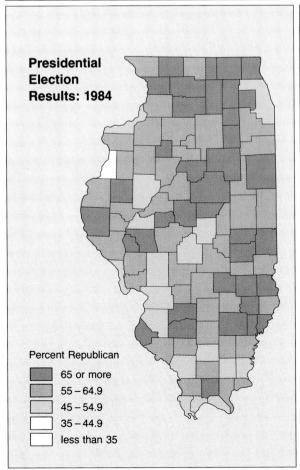

**Presidential
Election
Results: 1984**

Percent Republican

- 65 or more
- 55 – 64.9
- 45 – 54.9
- 35 – 44.9
- less than 35

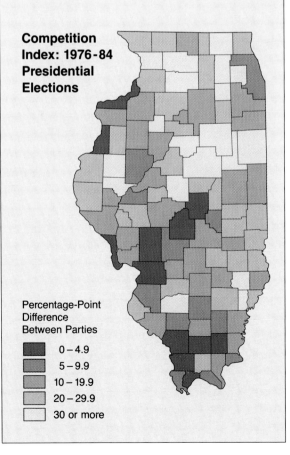

**Competition
Index: 1976-84
Presidential
Elections**

Percentage-Point
Difference
Between Parties

- 0 – 4.9
- 5 – 9.9
- 10 – 19.9
- 20 – 29.9
- 30 or more

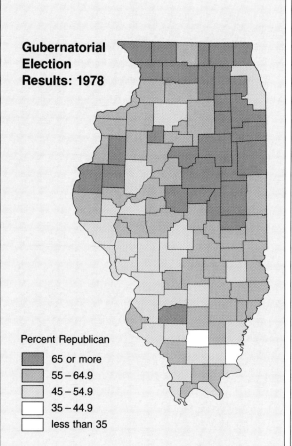

Gubernatorial Election Results: 1978

Percent Republican

- 65 or more
- 55 – 64.9
- 45 – 54.9
- 35 – 44.9
- less than 35

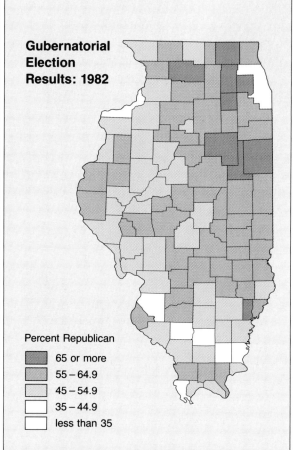

Gubernatorial Election Results: 1982

Percent Republican

- 65 or more
- 55 – 64.9
- 45 – 54.9
- 35 – 44.9
- less than 35

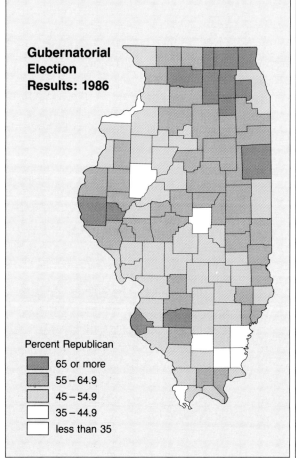

Gubernatorial Election Results: 1986

Percent Republican

- 65 or more
- 55 – 64.9
- 45 – 54.9
- 35 – 44.9
- less than 35

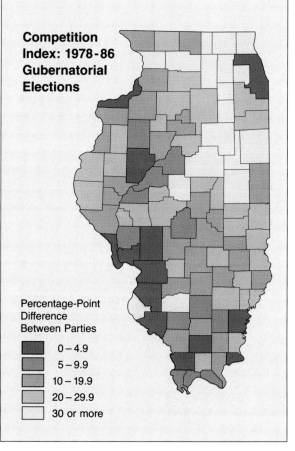

Competition Index: 1978-86 Gubernatorial Elections

Percentage-Point Difference Between Parties

- 0 – 4.9
- 5 – 9.9
- 10 – 19.9
- 20 – 29.9
- 30 or more

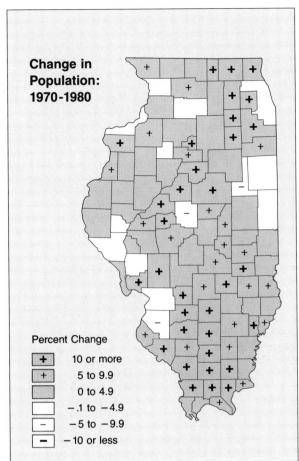

Change in Population: 1970-1980

Percent Change
- **+** 10 or more
- + 5 to 9.9
- (shaded) 0 to 4.9
- (white) −.1 to −4.9
- − −5 to −9.9
- **−** −10 or less

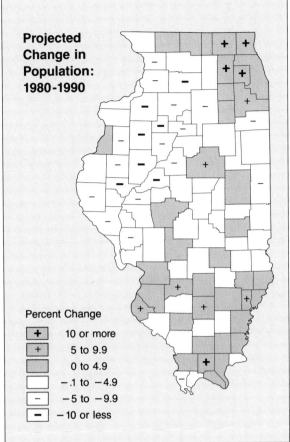

Projected Change in Population: 1980-1990

Percent Change
- **+** 10 or more
- + 5 to 9.9
- (shaded) 0 to 4.9
- (white) −.1 to −4.9
- − −5 to −9.9
- **−** −10 or less

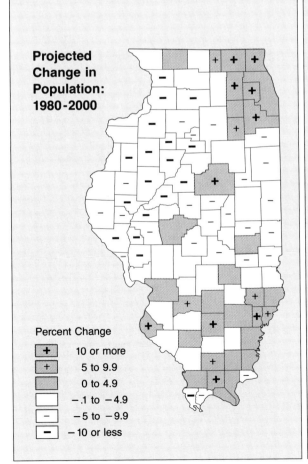

Projected Change in Population: 1980-2000

Percent Change
- **+** 10 or more
- + 5 to 9.9
- (shaded) 0 to 4.9
- (white) −.1 to −4.9
- − −5 to −9.9
- **−** −10 or less

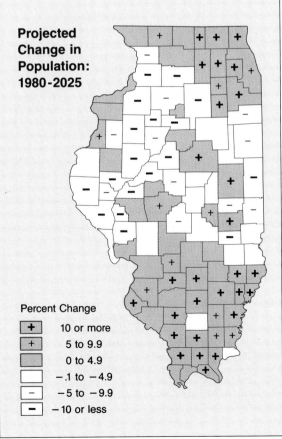

Projected Change in Population: 1980-2025

Percent Change
- **+** 10 or more
- + 5 to 9.9
- (shaded) 0 to 4.9
- (white) −.1 to −4.9
- − −5 to −9.9
- **−** −10 or less

75

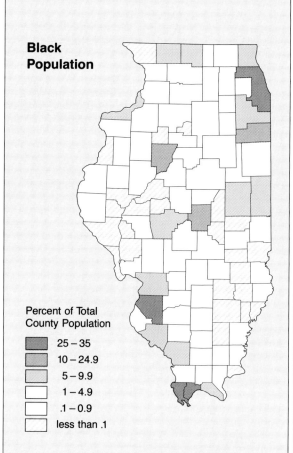

Black Population

Percent of Total County Population

- 25 – 35
- 10 – 24.9
- 5 – 9.9
- 1 – 4.9
- .1 – 0.9
- less than .1

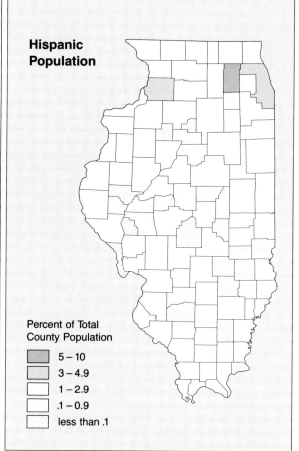

Hispanic Population

Percent of Total County Population

- 5 – 10
- 3 – 4.9
- 1 – 2.9
- .1 – 0.9
- less than .1

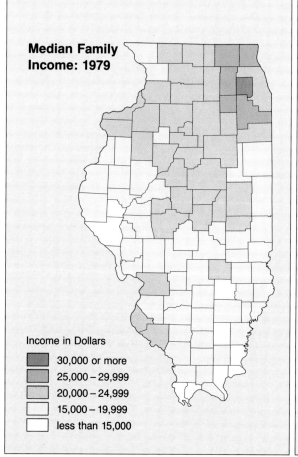

Median Family Income: 1979

Income in Dollars

- 30,000 or more
- 25,000 – 29,999
- 20,000 – 24,999
- 15,000 – 19,999
- less than 15,000

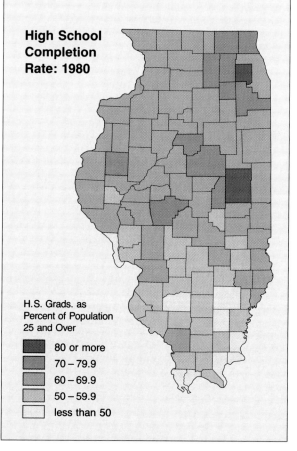

High School Completion Rate: 1980

H.S. Grads. as Percent of Population 25 and Over

- 80 or more
- 70 – 79.9
- 60 – 69.9
- 50 – 59.9
- less than 50

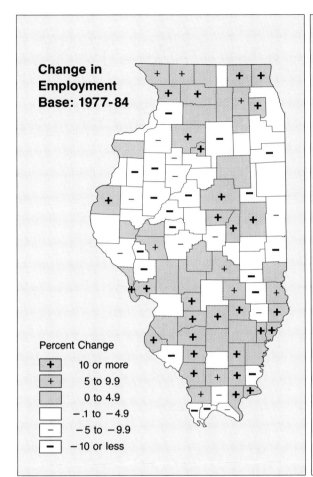

Change in Employment Base: 1977-84

Percent Change

+	10 or more
+	5 to 9.9
	0 to 4.9
	−.1 to −4.9
−	−5 to −9.9
—	−10 or less

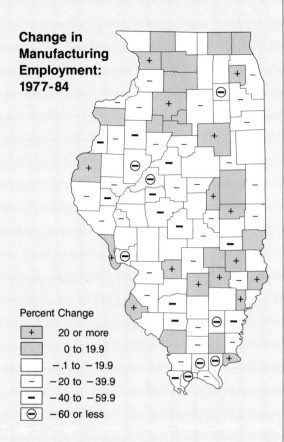

Change in Manufacturing Employment: 1977-84

Percent Change

+	20 or more
	0 to 19.9
	−.1 to −19.9
−	−20 to −39.9
—	−40 to −59.9
⊖	−60 or less

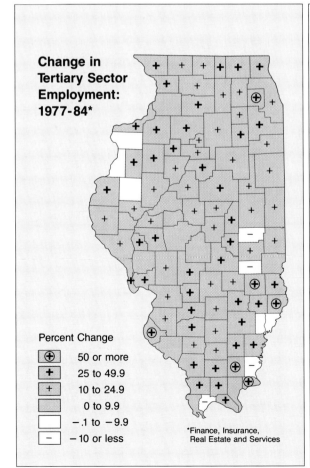

Change in Tertiary Sector Employment: 1977-84*

Percent Change

⊕	50 or more
+	25 to 49.9
+	10 to 24.9
	0 to 9.9
	−.1 to −9.9
−	−10 or less

*Finance, Insurance, Real Estate and Services

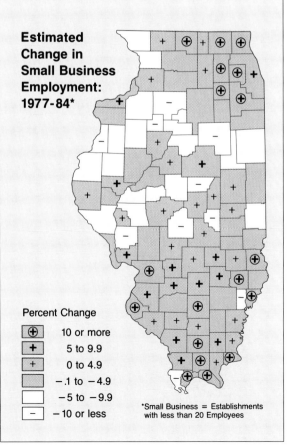

Estimated Change in Small Business Employment: 1977-84*

Percent Change

⊕	10 or more
+	5 to 9.9
+	0 to 4.9
	−.1 to −4.9
	−5 to −9.9
−	−10 or less

*Small Business = Establishments with less than 20 Employees

77

★ Chicago ★
S U M M A R Y
MAPS

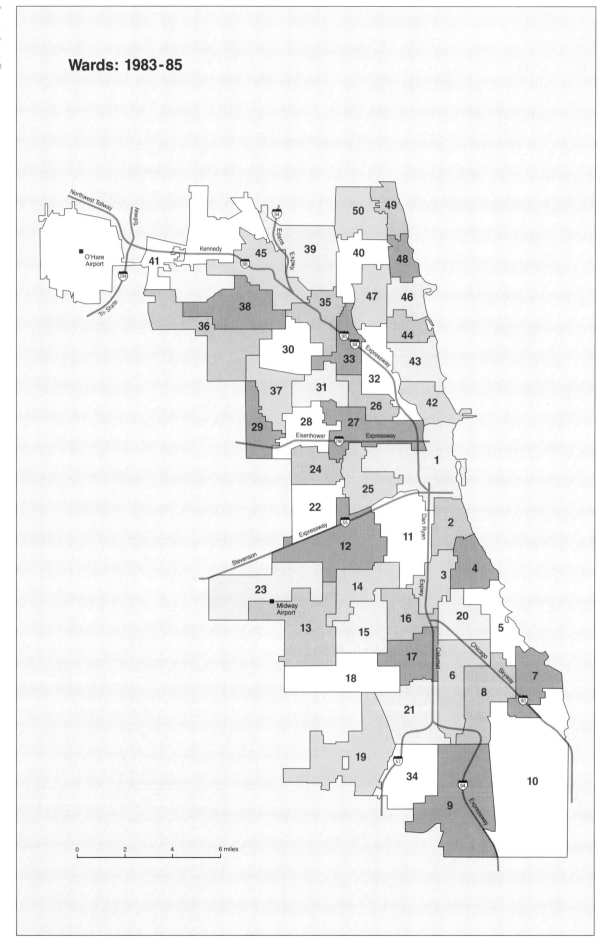

Wards: 1983-85

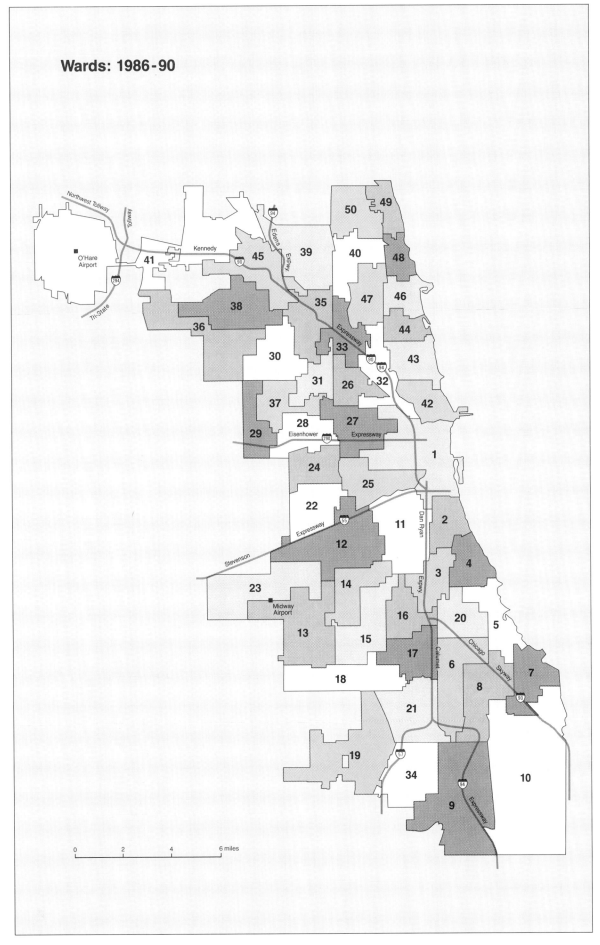

Wards: 1986-90

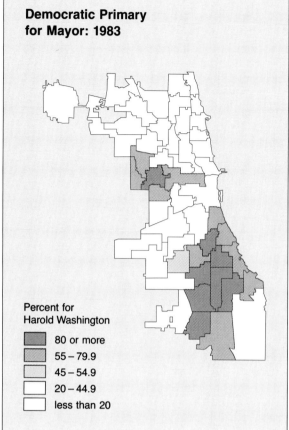

**Democratic Primary
for Mayor: 1983**

Percent for
Harold Washington

- 80 or more
- 55 – 79.9
- 45 – 54.9
- 20 – 44.9
- less than 20

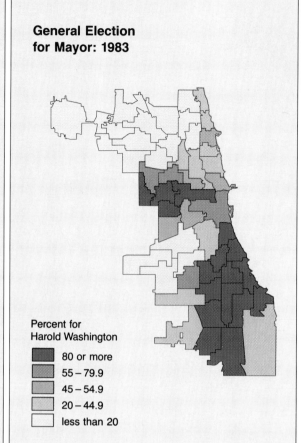

**General Election
for Mayor: 1983**

Percent for
Harold Washington

- 80 or more
- 55 – 79.9
- 45 – 54.9
- 20 – 44.9
- less than 20

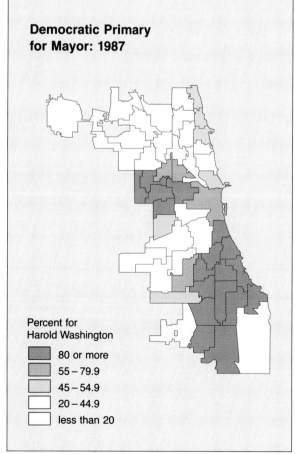

**Democratic Primary
for Mayor: 1987**

Percent for
Harold Washington

- 80 or more
- 55 – 79.9
- 45 – 54.9
- 20 – 44.9
- less than 20

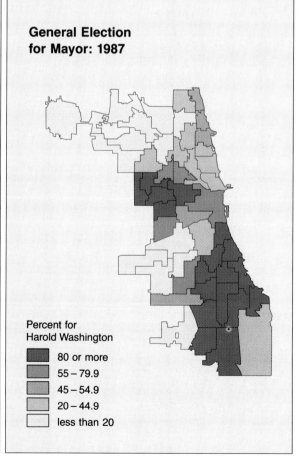

**General Election
for Mayor: 1987**

Percent for
Harold Washington

- 80 or more
- 55 – 79.9
- 45 – 54.9
- 20 – 44.9
- less than 20

·Chicago·

SUMMARY

Black Voting Age Population: 1983

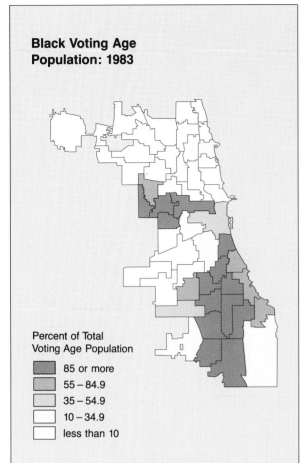

Percent of Total
Voting Age Population

- 85 or more
- 55 – 84.9
- 35 – 54.9
- 10 – 34.9
- less than 10

Hispanic Voting Age Population: 1983

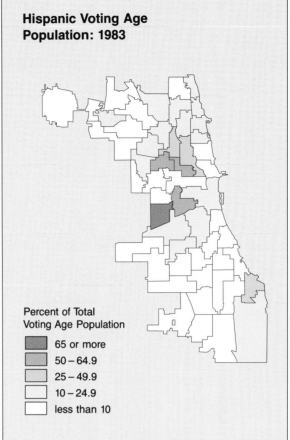

Percent of Total
Voting Age Population

- 65 or more
- 50 – 64.9
- 25 – 49.9
- 10 – 24.9
- less than 10

Black Voting Age Population: 1987

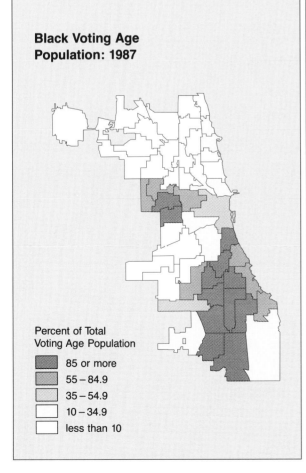

Percent of Total
Voting Age Population

- 85 or more
- 55 – 84.9
- 35 – 54.9
- 10 – 34.9
- less than 10

Hispanic Voting Age Population: 1987

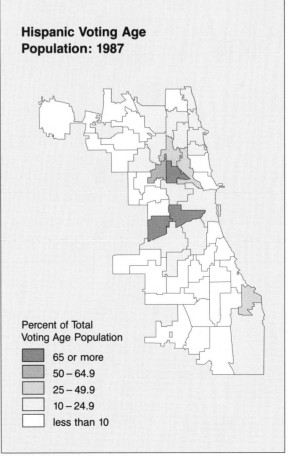

Percent of Total
Voting Age Population

- 65 or more
- 50 – 64.9
- 25 – 49.9
- 10 – 24.9
- less than 10

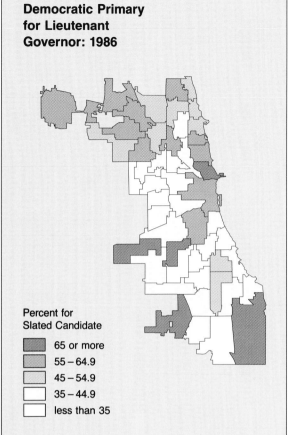

Democratic Primary for Lieutenant Governor: 1986

Percent for
Slated Candidate

- 65 or more
- 55 – 64.9
- 45 – 54.9
- 35 – 44.9
- less than 35

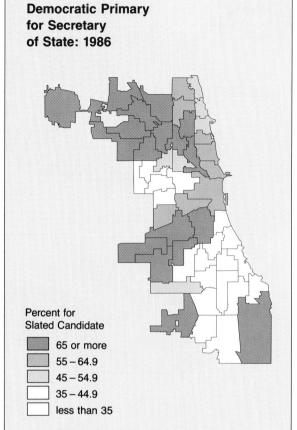

Democratic Primary for Secretary of State: 1986

Percent for
Slated Candidate

- 65 or more
- 55 – 64.9
- 45 – 54.9
- 35 – 44.9
- less than 35

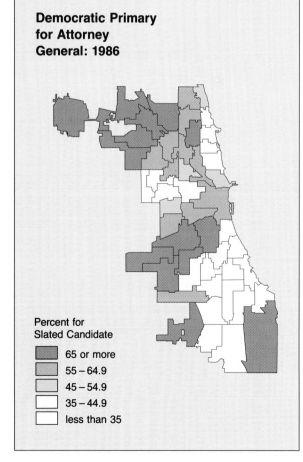

Democratic Primary for Attorney General: 1986

Percent for
Slated Candidate

- 65 or more
- 55 – 64.9
- 45 – 54.9
- 35 – 44.9
- less than 35

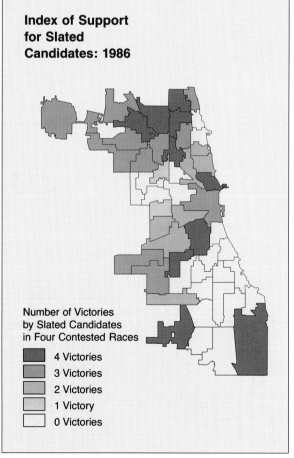

Index of Support for Slated Candidates: 1986

Number of Victories
by Slated Candidates
in Four Contested Races

- 4 Victories
- 3 Victories
- 2 Victories
- 1 Victory
- 0 Victories

·Chicago·
SUMMARY

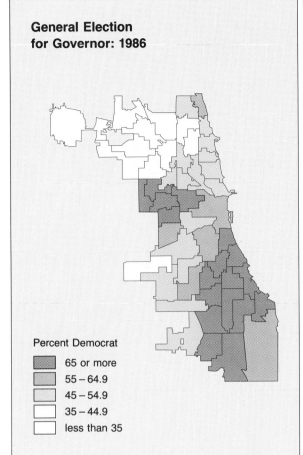

**General Election
for Governor: 1986**

Percent Democrat

- 65 or more
- 55 – 64.9
- 45 – 54.9
- 35 – 44.9
- less than 35

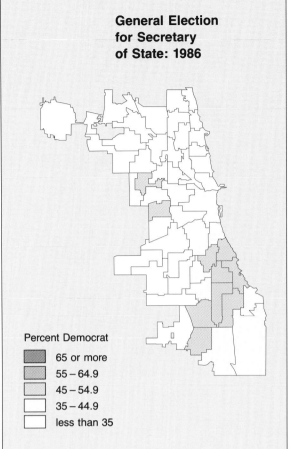

**General Election
for Secretary
of State: 1986**

Percent Democrat

- 65 or more
- 55 – 64.9
- 45 – 54.9
- 35 – 44.9
- less than 35

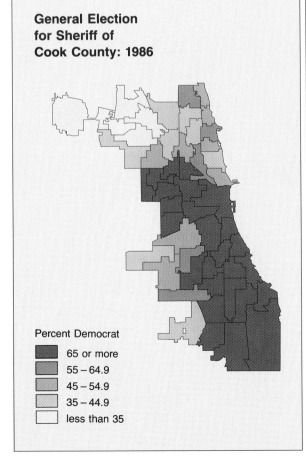

**General Election
for Sheriff of
Cook County: 1986**

Percent Democrat

- 65 or more
- 55 – 64.9
- 45 – 54.9
- 35 – 44.9
- less than 35

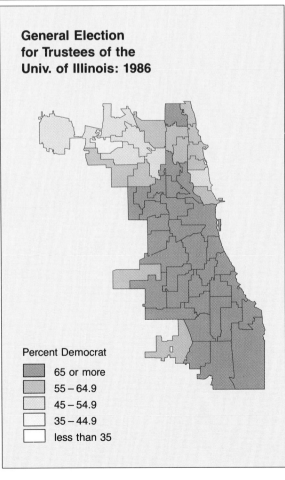

**General Election
for Trustees of the
Univ. of Illinois: 1986**

Percent Democrat

- 65 or more
- 55 – 64.9
- 45 – 54.9
- 35 – 44.9
- less than 35

85

Appendix I

Data Sources and Procedures

The demographic information reported in the statistical tables and maps was taken mainly from the 1980 U. S. Census, Summary Tape File 1 (STF1) and Summary Tape File 3 (STF3), and from the County Business Patterns annual files. The Illinois Bureau of the Budget, Division of Planning and Financial Analysis, provided the county-level population projections, and the Boards of Elections for the city of Chicago and the state of Illinois supplied the election data.

We followed several steps to develop two files of matched census and political data, one containing 118 cases corresponding to the state's house districts and a second file for the 59 senate districts. First, to identify the blocks, tracts, townships, or counties that fell into each of the 118 house districts, we drew boundaries for each district onto a set of census maps, following the written descriptions and outline maps provided by the Illinois Board of Elections. Second, we created a district affiliation list, using as a base a computer-readable list of county, township, tract, and block numbers written out from the U. S. Census. Third, we matched this district affiliation list against data files containing the census variables and aggregated the approximately eighty thousand blocks, tracts, and townships in the state up to the house district level. Finally, since each senate district consists of two adjacent house districts, we created a senate file by aggregating the data contained in the house file.

We took the data for voting age population by race or ethnic group, urban population, and housing from STF1. The data for population by age and education, families, and industrial employment came from STF3. The reported totals were used to calculate the individual percentages for each category. These percentages may not sum to 100 percent because we have not always reported every possible subgroup. For example, the employment data exclude persons employed in agriculture and construction, but an aggregate percentage for these two groups can be obtained by subtracting the sum of the reported categories from one hundred.

A few variables require some additional explanation. *Urban population* refers to the number of persons residing in places of greater than 2,500 people. The proportion of owner-occupied housing excludes condominiums and houses sited on ten or more acres. The education variables report the percentages of people age twenty-five and above who completed up to eleven years of schools but did not graduate from high school and those who completed four or more years of college.

Presenting both median family income and the median value of housing required manipulation of the original census data. Since the census only reports these items as categorical values for groups of blocks to protect the identity of individuals, we applied the standard formula for calculating measures of central tendency from categorical data. For the same reason, we had to calculate these values separately for the house and senate districts.

For the ethnic data presented as sidebar information for some districts, the Asian category includes individuals reporting their ancestry as Japanese, Chinese, Filipino, Korean, Vietnamese, or Asian-Indian. Southern and Eastern Europeans are those of Greek, Hungarian, Italian, Portugese, Russian, or Ukranian origin; and Northern and Western Europeans are those whose ancestry is English, Irish, Scottish, Welsh, French, German, Norwegian, or Swedish.

Finally, we calculated the competition index arrayed on some of the summary maps by taking the absolute difference between the percentage of the vote cast for the Democrats and for the Republicans.

Appendix II

General Election Results for Senate Districts—1986

	Democratic			Republican	
District	Candidate	Vote		Candidate	Vote
2	Arthur L. Berman	36,105		Lee A. Leichentritt	13,191
3	William A. Marovitz	33,040		David E. Riley	13,009
5	Miguel Del Valle	23,796		Wayne M. Haney	5,868
6	Thaddeus (Ted) Lechowicz	32,882		Chester R. Hornowski	9,916
8	Philip J. Rock	44,520		No Candidate	——
9	Earlean Collins	33,384		Harry E. Johnson	7,860
11	Timothy F. Degnan	34,191		Clement J. Balonek	9,123
12	Margaret Smith	34,781		Jackie Brown	1,637
14	Jeremiah E. Joyce	41,871		Donald W. Walsh	18,432
15	Frank D. Savickas	50,263		David J. Smith	18,800
16	Ethel Skyles Alexander	45,776		No Candidate	——
17	Emil Jones, Jr.	41,059		Daniel J. Olofsson	7,867
18	Howard B. Brookins	55,030		Steven Jerome Kay	5,257
20	Daniel T. Smyth	15,930		Beverly Fawell	39,663
21	No Candidate	——		Forest D. Etheredge	39,609
23	No Candidate	——		James (Pate) Philip	38,658
24	LeRoy Walter Lemke	29,366		Robert M. Raica	35,420
26	Greg Zito	34,707		Vic Pilolla	13,960
27	No Candidate	——		Virginia B. MacDonald	41,983
29	Burton I. Weinstein	24,155		Roger A. Keats	36,806
30	No Candidate	——		David N. Barkhausen	42,903
32	No Candidate	——		Jack Schaffer	46,100
33	Charles A. Marwig	11,038		John E. Friedland	34,910
35	No Candidate	——		Harlan Rigney	45,323
36	Denny Jacobs	34,529		H. (Bud) Ford	19,183
38	Patrick D. Welch	29,984		Thomas C. Setchell	28,076
39	Richard F. Kelly, Jr.	28,062		Peter Liaka	12,170

District	Candidate (D)	Vote	Candidate (R)	Vote
41	Gregory N. Freerksen	14,020	George (Ray) Hudson	37,647
42	Thomas A. Dunn	25,414	John Bourg	21,144
44	No Candidate	——	John W. Maitland, Jr.	43,737
45	Bobby Rhines	13,556	Robert A. Madigan	45,924
47	John E. (Jack) Cassidy, Jr.	20,380	Carl E. Hawkinson	36,564
48	Hubert G. Staff	25,578	Laura Kent Donahue	37,586
50	Sam Cahnman	31,159	John A. Davidson	49,406
51	Penny L. Severns	31,646	James H. Rupp	27,576
53	Alan D. Holderfield	21,959	Harry (Babe) Woodyard	8,452
54	William L. O'Daniel	41,550	Charles J. Carpentier	30,875
56	Sam M. Vadalabene	37,039	No Candidate	——
57	Kenneth Hall	33,235	No Candidate	——
59	Glenn Poshard	55,207	Richard Simmons	21,855

Appendix III

General Election Results for Representative Districts—1986

	Democratic		Republican	
District	Candidate	Vote	Candidate	Vote
1	Alan J. Greiman	20,162	Kenneth H. Hollander	10,204
2	William J. Laurino	19,249	Fawn V. Hurst	7,365
3	Lee Preston	18,653	Jerry Ex	4,839
4	Woody Bowman	17,388	Jonathan M. Walker	8,000
5	Ellis B. Levin	16,341	Carol J. Dannenhauer	6,083
6	Bruce A. Farley	13,135	Virginia V. Mann	7,112
7	John J. Cullerton	16,654	Cornelius J. Tanis	5,189
8	Jesse C. White, Jr.	17,456	Marshall R. Crawford	11,114
9	Joseph Berrios	12,146	No Candidate	——
10	Myron J. Kulas	12,708	Dennis F. Villare	2,381
11	Robert (Bob) Bugielski	16,969	No Candidate	——
12	Alfred G. Ronan	13,945	Warren W. Sikorski	5,404
13	Ralph C. Capparelli	24,804	Carol Panek	14,047
14	Robert S. Wronski	12,117	Roger P. McAuliffe	21,054
15	Robert LeFlore, Jr.	16,500	Margaret S. Cartwright	3,525
16	James A. DeLeo	21,328	Mary E. Fickenscher	12,624
17	Anthony L. Young	15,752	Marie T. Pikul	4,270
18	Arthur L. Turner	16,733	George Johnson	3,670
19	Douglas Huff, Jr.	16,830	Charles (Chuck) Mobley	2,855
20	Ben Martinez	8,844	Fernando Murillo	1,274
21	John P. Daley	18,825	Marjorie Ann Hoeller	2,267
22	Robert T. Krska	16,749	George Esch	5,928
23	Lovana S. (Lou) Jones	16,947	A. A. (Sammy) Rayner, Jr.	1,787
24	Paul L. Williams	16,069	Marvella Stewart	688
25	Carol Moseley Braun	24,187	Billie Jean Buckley	1,103
26	Barbara Flynn Currie	22,781	Archietta Shannon	977
27	John J. McNamara	15,938	Annette Dixon	7,900

District	Candidate (D)	Vote	Candidate (R)	Vote
28	James F. Keane	26,343	John Peter O'Toole	9,673
29	Andrew J. McGann	21,899	Tom McAvoy	12,257
30	Michael J. Madigan	27,954	Stanley C. Sobrya	7,580
31	Mary E. Flowers	20,778	Mildred J. Thompson	622
32	Charles G. Morrow III	23,129	Paulette Anderson	980
33	Nelson Rice, Sr.	20,816	John Allen	4,339
34	William (Bill) Shaw	19,512	Robert H. Anderson	3,558
35	Samuel Panayotovich	25,698	Matthew J. Baker	2,920
36	Monique D. Davis	30,790	Direoce Anthony Junirs	804
37	No Candidate	——	Loleta A. Didrickson	23,030
38	Dagmar F. Johnson	6,431	Jane M. Barnes	22,144
39	No Candidate	——	Ralph H. Barger	23,170
40	Truman Kirkpatrick	8,390	Gene L. Hoffman	20,131
41	No Candidate	——	Mary Lou Cowlishaw	20,960
42	Thomas E. Blake	6,966	Suzanne L. (Sue) Deuchler	16,122
43	Russell W. Hartigan	11,468	Jack L. Kubik	20,314
44	Mary Jo Noonan	9,114	James R. Stange	22,271
45	No Candidate	——	Kathleen L. (Kay) Wojcik	18,743
46	No Candidate	——	Lee A. Daniels	20,171
47	John T. O'Connell	13,518	Anne S. Zickus	13,280
48	Robert M. Terzich	21,139	Phillip Bianco, Jr.	15,804
49	Ronald G. Bobkowski	5,618	Terry R. Parke	12,675
50	Michael Leo Sanders	6,801	Donald N. Hensel	18,777
51	Ted E. Leverenz	17,321	John R. Spaulding	6,780
52	Geoffrey S. Obrzut	10,960	Linda Williamson	12,743
53	Kenneth A. Cook, Jr.	5,775	David Harris	15,946
54	No Candidate	——	Bernard E. Pedersen	21,426
55	Diana Burgess Sheffer	6,963	Penny Pullen	21,432
56	Calvin R. Sutker	15,537	Sheldon Marcus	14,024
57	Denise Hertz McGrath	7,465	Margaret R. Parcells	25,050
58	Grace Mary Stern	18,479	Robert B. Jans	9,190
59	No Candidate	——	Virginia Fiester Frederick	22,078
60	No Candidate	——	William E. Peterson	20,972
61	John S. Matijevich	8,680	John E. Bobel	3,177

District	Candidate (D)	Vote	Candidate (R)	Vote
62	No Candidate	——	Robert W. Churchill	16,088
63	No Candidate	——	Dick Klemm	23,343
64	No Candidate	——	Ronald A. Wait	22,370
65	No Candidate	——	DeLoris Doederlein	20,792
66	No Candidate	——	James M. Kirkland	19,635
67	No Candidate	——	John W. Hallock, Jr.	22,516
68	E. J. (Zeke) Giorgi	13,675	Robert A. Pfluger	6,917
69	Richard T. (Dick) Mulcahey	18,457	Mark B. McLeRoy	12,310
70	No Candidate	——	Myron J. Olson	21,022
71	Joel D. Brunsvold	19,605	E. R. (Dick) Friesth	6,767
72	M. (Bob) DeJaegher	17,283	Michael Roche	9,960
73	Joseph Leo Miller	9,068	Todd Sieben	19,940
74	Richard A. Mautino	19,092	Dan Whitlock	9,019
75	Peg McDonnell Breslin	25,929	No Candidate	——
76	Greg Sparrow	9,905	John Countryman	16,164
77	Frank Giglio	13,059	Gene (Wojciechowski) Wolfe	8,739
78	Terry A. Steczo	15,190	No Candidate	——
79	Alfred R. Ragonese	7,744	Robert J. Piel	16,081
80	Jim Marzuki	9,844	Robert P. Regan	12,724
81	Paul S. Farber	6,617	Thomas J. McCracken, Jr.	19,635
82	No Candidate	——	Edward F. Petka	22,139
83	LeRoy Van Duyne	12,600	Joseph M. Jenco	10,070
84	Charles R. Adelman	10,852	Larry Wennlund	11,967
85	Ray A. Christensen	14,213	Gerald (Jerry) C. Weller	14,217
86	Charles (Chuck) Pangle	17,469	Charles (Chuck) Henderson	9,008
87	Lloyd Metz	6,991	Thomas W. Ewing	20,951
88	Kenneth S. McCrady	5,511	Gordon L. Ropp	18,277
89	No Candidate	——	Jay Ackerman	22,263
90	No Candidate	——	Robert F. Olson	25,880
91	Thomas J. Homer	17,433	Donna L. Woodrow	6,544
92	Donald L. Saltsman	12,538	Daniel A. LaKemper	5,396
93	Tim Bertschy	12,793	Fred J. Tuerk	14,612
94	Samuel M. McGrew	13,766	David Hultgren	15,340
95	George A. Lipper	11,452	Kent Slater	17,731

District	Candidate (D)	Vote	Candidate (R)	Vote
96	Robert E. Summey	15,033	Jeff Mays	18,398
97	Charles K. Barnett	12,968	Tom Ryder	22,582
98	Gary Hannig	17,507	Becky Doyle	16,312
99	Michael Curran	22,786	Bob Nika	17,901
100	Don Huddleston	19,561	Karen Hasara	21,101
101	John F. Dunn	18,557	Lee O. Sturgis, Sr.	7,100
102	No Candidate	——	Michael J. Tate	24,819
103	Helen F. Satterthwaite	12,985	Brian C. Silverman	8,237
104	Jerry Stout	7,804	Timothy V. Johnson	18,986
105	Larry R. Stuffle	13,999	William B. Black	15,468
106	Boyd Davis	9,173	Michael (Mike) Weaver	21,626
107	Charles A. (Chuck) Hartke	23,952	Gerald C. Harper	11,523
108	Larry W. Hicks	23,766	Cecil L. Wyant	12,618
109	Kurt M. Granberg	18,349	Dwight P. Friedrich	16,297
110	Michael (Mike) Slape	9,770	Ron Stephens	15,450
111	Sam W. Wolf	16,087	Kevin W. Sykes	6,885
112	Jim McPike	17,055	No Candidate	——
113	Wyvetter H. Younge	13,529	Winston V. Springer	5,545
114	Monroe L. Flinn	13,572	Robert M. (Bob) Goins	9,357
115	Jerry K. Thomas	15,276	Charles Wayne Goforth	19,671
116	Bruce Richmond	20,175	Herman F. Wright	9,239
117	James F. (Jim) Rea	25,768	Doris L. Boynton	11,429
118	David D. Phelps	23,354	Guy Lahr	16,929